# Social Media Campaigns

Social media has ushered in a new era of communication between organizations and key stakeholders. This text guides readers through a four-step process of developing a robust social media campaign. Covering the latest industry standards and best practices to engage digital audiences through social listening, strategic design, creative engagement and evaluation, each chapter also includes expert insights from social media professionals. Focusing on principles rather than a specific platform, this is a text dedicated to developing social media competency that can adapt to any organization or environment.

**Carolyn Mae Kim** is an assistant professor of public relations at Biola University. Her research specialties include credibility, digital strategy, media ecology, and public relations education.

# Social Media Campaigns

## Strategies for Public Relations and Marketing

Carolyn Mae Kim

Routledge
Taylor & Francis Group

NEW YORK AND LONDON

First published 2016
by Routledge
711 Third Avenue, New York, NY 10017

and by Routledge
2 Park Square, Milton Park, Abingdon, Oxon, OX14 4RN

*Routledge is an imprint of the Taylor & Francis Group, an informa business*

© 2016 Taylor & Francis

*Library of Congress Cataloging in Publication Data*
Names: Kim, Carolyn Mae, author.
Title: Social media campaigns : strategies for public relations and marketing
/ Carolyn Mae Kim.
Description: New York, NY : Routledge, 2016. | Includes index.
Identifiers: LCCN 2015048433 (print) | LCCN 2016004224 (ebook) |
ISBN 9781138948594 (hardback) | ISBN 9781138948600 (pbk.) |
ISBN 9781315652375 (ebook)
Subjects: LCSH: Internet in public relations. | Internet marketing. |
Social media. | Public relations.
Classification: LCC HD59 .K558 2016 (print) | LCC HD59 (ebook) |
DDC 658.8/72—dc23

ISBN: [978-1-138-94859-4] (hbk)
ISBN: [978-1-138-94860-0] (pbk)
ISBN: [978-1-315-65237-5] (ebk)

Typeset in Sabon
by Keystroke, Station Road, Codsall, Wolverhampton

# Contents

# Illustrations

# Dedication and Acknowledgments

This book is dedicated to my incredible husband, KiYong Kim. Because of his championing, I took a chance and submitted a book proposal. Because of his editing and brainstorming, I managed to complete this text. Throughout countless walks discussing social media campaigns and weekends packed with editing and feedback, he never wavered in his support and encouragement. This would never have been possible without him.

I also am indebted to my colleague, mentor, and friend, Karen Freberg, for her inspiration, support, and encouragement throughout this journey. She is a paramount educator and professional to whom I'm incredibly grateful. Additionally, I am so deeply appreciative of my family, friends, and colleagues who listened, advised, and cheered me on through this process. There are no words that fully capture the value of what each of these individuals contributed. In addition, my truly outstanding students inspired me to write this text through their enthusiastic support and excitement for the world of social media.

Finally, I would like to thank the professionals who gave of their time to participate in the expert insights, providing industry perspectives from which students could learn. They made an incredibly valuable contribution for which I am exceedingly grateful!

# Social Media Campaigns at a Glance

**Social Influence**

- *Understanding the development, value, and role of social media for organizations*

**Step 1: Listening**

- *Developing research, discovering data, and applying meaning*

**Step 2: Strategic Design**

- *Developing a data-informed social media campaign*
- *Designing creative engagement in brand communities*

**Step 3: Implementation and Monitoring**

- *Joining conversations and creating purposeful interaction*

**Step 4: Evaluation**

- *Showcasing success and growth opportunities*

# Chapter 1

# Social Influence

## Understanding the Development, Value, and Role of Social Media for Organizations

Organizations are operating in a new, social paradigm. Brands can no longer expect to control, dictate, or push a conversation onto the public. Rather, they must engage with the public, creating a two-way, relevant conversation in order to thrive in today's social world.

Social media has changed the fabric of society. With more mobile devices connected to the Internet than there are people in the world, the impact of social media is felt in every facet of culture (Bennett, 2013). In the world of public relations, marketing, and communication, it is more important than ever that professionals have a strategic understanding of how to utilize social media effectively. Having a purposeful design to social media has the potential to ignite powerful conversations among key stakeholders. As social media has developed as a platform, and organizations have matured in their approach to social media community engagement, the methodology to using social media as a platform also needs to change. While every organization, online community, and social media campaign will have its own unique flavor, there is, nevertheless, a unifying model that underlies social media campaigns, which fosters strategic engagement. This model provides a framework on which all the creative, individualized approaches to social relationships can take shape. Organizations that get the most success from social media campaigns, however, not only understand the process of a social media campaign but also the way social media should integrate into the entire organization's ethos.

## Social Organizational Culture

There is a significant difference between brands that infuse social strategies into the entire organization, and those that use them only in social media campaigns for communication purposes. Michael Brito (2014) differentiates these two concepts as a "social brand" versus a "social business strategy." While a social brand uses social technologies to communicate

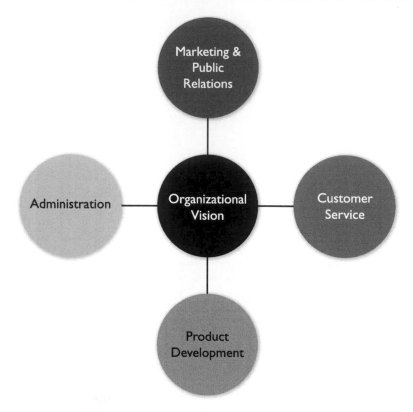

*Figure 1.1* The Historical Business Model

with their key audiences, a social business strategy is a "documented plan of action that helps evolve and transform the thinking of an organization bridging internal and external social initiatives resulting in collaborative connections, a more social organization, and shared value for all stakeholders" (p. 44). Figure 1.1 illustrates what a historical approach to a business model looks like. Each department in the organization is separated by their individual roles, responsibilities, and objectives. While they all jointly support the success of the business, they individually specialize in only their specific purpose.

Today's business environment, however, is not a static process that can approach key stakeholders in a mechanized way with each department solely responsible for only their area. Departments can no longer function in a silo without interacting with each other to support the needs of key relationships. Publics expect brands to be holistic, connecting across multiple departments and with multiple people in order to provide the best solution for each stakeholder's need. For example, if someone contacts the brand through Twitter about a concern with billing or with a product, it is important that the social media team communicates *with* the other department in order to get an answer and respond to the individual. Simply giving the phone number or email number of the other department to the person on Twitter, instead of providing the answer, gives the impression that interaction between departments does not occur. The message that is being sent, then, is that the business is not actually relational *internally*, but simply wants to give the impression that it is relational. Today's social business is all about connecting and relating, both *internally* with others in the organization and externally with audiences and their needs. This model is illustrated in Figure 1.2, which shows how the various departments not only surround and support the vision of the brand, but also help each other. *Social organizations* are brands that recognize social interaction as a *core approach* to business rather than social media as a *tool* to accomplish business, and thus experience the power of authentic relationships with key stakeholders.

*Figure 1.2* The Social Business Model

For a brand to be social requires an entire paradigm shift in business and structure. Jay Baer (2013) points out that organizations need to now operate in a "friend-of-mine awareness," recognizing that, in today's world, people do business with brands with which they have relationships. "Like never before in the history of business, our personal and commercial relationships are merging and entangling, line for line, pixel for pixel" (p. 27). He goes on to describe an approach that he has named "Youtility."

> Youtility is marketing upside down. Instead of marketing that's needed by companies, Youtility is marketing that's wanted by customers. Youtility is massively useful information, provided for free, that creates long-term trust and kinship between your company and customers. The difference between helping and selling is just two letters. But those two letters now make all the difference.
>
> (p. 3)

In order to achieve this Youtility approach to an organization, Baer (2013) suggests that organizations have to recognize that publics want self-serve information, allowing them to get all the details they need whenever they are looking for them. In addition, they expect brands to operate with radical transparency, giving answers and information before they are asked for, and real-time relevancy, which utilizes technology and engagement to connect with key stakeholders in meaningful ways (p. 44). Essentially, the new paradigm of business in today's social world is all about people. We need to go back to the basics, valuing and investing in relationships with people connected to our brand. For a brand to truly be social, therefore, people have to matter: at every level and in every decision. Social organizations do not just use social media as a tool to communicate. Social organizations operate in an entirely different framework than historical models—they operate in a *social paradigm of business,* placing people and their needs/desires/values front and center in business operations and decisions. Social media, then, should serve as an indicator of the relational priorities of the brand within the digital world, not as the only source of relational interaction that occurs within the organization.

### The Crisis of Trust

People do business with organizations that they trust . . . with *people* that they trust. In a world with more competition than ever before, and thousands of options for people to choose from, relationship becomes the defining factor in business. Unfortunately, despite trust being the cornerstone for ongoing relationships with key stakeholders, there are countless examples of organizations that have defrauded and lied to the public. This broken trust and lack of transparency within business has led to a deep-seated distrust of organizations by the public. The Crisis of Trust can be defined as the developing belief that organizations are deceitful or inauthentic in their communication and relationship with the public. Rohit Bhargava (2012) identified this issue as the believability crisis. Bhargava traced the development of our "society of distrust" by exploring the role of propaganda, unethical marketing and public relations and the introduction of mass communication to overwhelm marketplaces with those who could pay the most to have the loudest voice. This method, ultimately, ended up treating people like commodities rather than valued relationships. With trust in all institutions at an all-time low, "people are less likely to trust anyone or anything" (p. 17). He suggests that when communication is humanized, focusing on individuals and relationships, three important elements are reintroduced: purpose, empowerment, and appreciation. The developing of this personal relationship through these three elements has the power to rebuild trust between brands and the public (p. 25). In conclusion, while brands today are operating in a time of deep mistrust by the public, due to the unethical and harmful practices that have come to light in the last several decades, social organizations are able to directly counter the believability crisis by building meaningful and authentic relationships with individuals. This commitment to relationships that provide value and are built on trust is the heart of the Social Principle.

## The Social Principle

A key tenet of social media engagement is relationships. Social engagement is driven out of connection and community. When organizations enter the social environment, they must keep these facts in mind to be effective in social spaces. Social media is not just a tool—it is a tangible expression of an organizational commitment to trust and value in relationships that is the heart of the social principle. The *social principle* is simply this: the fluid nature of social media is designed for and sustained in *relationship* through two-way communication around topics of mutual interest that is user-initiated, -created, and -driven. When organizations realize that social media is not a publicity tool used to plaster information in front of users, but rather a dynamic communication platform to foster two-way relationships in an unscripted environment, they are positioned to truly ignite their social communities.

In order to fully explore the social media model in today's organizational environment, it is helpful to understand how online communities developed. Equipped with an understanding of the background and history of how brand communities and organizations on social media have advanced, as well as what has led to developing relationships in social spaces, the full value of this book's proposed social media model will take on much more meaning.

**EXPERT INSIGHT**

*Karen Freberg, Ph.D.*

**What do you think is one hallmark competency social media professionals need to succeed?**

Writing is absolutely key. However, it's not just about writing in one platform, but evolving your writing skills to fit the platforms as they change. Plus, we have to look at writing in different circumstances and timing. Social media is a real-time form of media, so we have to be able to write content effectively in a few hours to a few seconds.

**What are some key considerations for brands on social media who want to be effective?**

Planning and strategy are still at the heart of what makes brands successful on social media. You do not have to be on all platforms, but you want to be there to engage on the platforms where your audiences are located and communicating on. It's about preparing for various situations and being creative yet strategic in how you approach each situation.

**With the constantly changing landscape of social media, how can organizations stay relevant?**

Social media is a living, breathing platform, and brands have to continue to educate themselves to be on top of the growing changes and shifts we are seeing in the field. Building a strong community of influencers and educators to help share knowledge and trends with each other is essential to stay ahead of the game as well.

**Why do you think social media is so powerful in today's culture?**

Social media has allowed the individual user to bypass gatekeepers to formulate their own media channel. We are able to share content and connect with people in real-time and break down the traditional barriers of communication that have been around for decades. While there are lots of great opportunities that make social media powerful, we also have to consider the challenges it has raised and how it is a powerful, and sometimes dangerous, platform and community. It's about understanding the balance of what makes social media powerful—the positives and the negatives.

**What are some of the biggest challenges for brands when they build brand communities in social media?**

I'd say trying to be something you are not. It's about being true to your values and unique characteristics as a company and brand that is appealing to people. Audiences want brands who are authentic and transparent with their actions and communication. It's not all about promotion and one-way communication, rather that it's really about being active, engaged, and listening to be part of the dialogue. Social media is interactive, so if brands establish themselves on a particular platform, they have to be engaged and invested in formulating and developing the community. Also, brands have to recognize if they are on social media platforms, they are essentially on rented property (e.g. Facebook, Instagram, Twitter, Snapchat). We have to follow the rules, terms of service agreements, and changes that follow on the platform. Engaging on these platforms is one thing, but realize you have to have an integrated approach that balances shared/earned media along with owned and paid media.

**What does it take for a brand to truly be social?**

Social media is indeed a lifestyle, and a brand that embraces this throughout their company and among their employees is going to be successful. I have seen brands that are as engaged online as they are offline. This is one thing I do look for when it comes to strong social media communities and examples to share with my students in the classroom. It comes down to the time, effort, and investment digital and social media managers have put into the social landscape. I have to say there are several brands who excel in this arena like Hootsuite, Sprout Social, GM, Skype, and Under Armour. However, sports organizations and teams are ones who I look to as strong examples of embracing social media throughout the organization, community, and team. Teams like the Dallas Mavericks, Team USA, Golden State Warriors, USA FIFA Women's World Cup team, XGames University of Nebraska, and Oklahoma Sooners are pretty exceptional in how they have embraced this.

**How can social media teams work to minimize crisis or brand risk within social media?**

Great question! I think it comes down to crisis prevention and planning. Social media is changing and we have to look at the potential good and challenging situations that can arise online. There are some situations we can't always plan for, but there are others we can, so it is important to educate, train, and implement these proactive practices before an issue transforms to a crisis online.

**Connect with Karen:** @kfreberg | https://www.linkedin.com/in/karenfreberg | https://www.facebook.com/karen.freberg

*Karen Freberg is an Assistant Professor at the University of Louisville and adjunct instructor for the Integrated Marketing Communications Graduate Online Program for West Virginia University*

## Developing and Defining Online Communities

The online world has brought in a new focus for public relations and marketing—social media communities, or non-geographically bound groups of people connected through a common social media platform. Much of the world is now connected within and across online communities through various social media platforms. In one of the first studies dealing with online communities, Rheingold (2000) pointed out that the concept of a virtual world is nothing new. In fact, in 1968, researchers for the Department of Defense's Advanced Research Projects Agency (DARPA) initiated what would become the first online community and the Internet: ARPANET. These DARPA researchers speculated that communities in the future would not depend on geographic location but rather on common interests (2000, p. 9). This is exactly what the current culture of social media embodies. People can create online communities, or what Seth Godin (2008) coined as "tribes." A tribe is "a group of people connected to one another, connected to a leader, and connected to an idea. . . . A group needs only two things to be a tribe: a shared interest and a way to communicate" (pp. 1–2). With the Internet, the ability to connect and have shared interests and ideas is easier than ever. There is no longer a need to depend on a physical, geographic location in order to form communities of people interested in a common focus. Instead, webs of connections form virtually as people interact in social environments on the Internet.

Rheingold (2000) defines virtual communities as "social aggregations that emerge from the Net when enough people carry on those public discussions with sufficient human feeling, to form webs of personal relationships in Cyberspace" (p. 5). This is an important definition as it focuses on the idea that the very fabric of an online community is the development of personal relationships. Social media's power emerged from and is sustained through personal connection. Bagozzi and Dholakia (2002) further clarify the term "virtual communities," with the definition of "mediated social spaces in the digital environment that allow groups to form and be sustained primarily through ongoing communication processes" (p. 3). As with the previous definition, this articulation of a virtual community high-lights engagement and sustained two-way communication. Many similar definitions hit on the main concepts of the Internet being a space utilized by individuals to form relationships and communicate with others in the social community. Additionally, studies have shown that the top incentives to join virtual communities are the desire for information exchange, social support, friendship, and recreation (Ridings & Gefen, 2004, pp. 6–10). The primary motivation for people from those four motivators is the desire for information exchange (Ridings & Gefen, 2004, p. 28).

While brands recognize that social media is a place to share information and to build connections within a community, there often seems to be confusion on what qualifies specifically as *social* media. Before one can strategically design a campaign *for* social media, one must be able to define social media. This places limits and parameters on what will be included within a *social media* campaign, as it specifies the type of technology, platform, and communities that social media campaigns will engage.

### Social Media Defined

To help differentiate what qualifies as *social* media, versus *new* media or *emerging* media or *wearable* media, it is helpful to refer to a definition given by Boyd and Ellison (2007). They defined social networking sites (social media) as:

> Web-based services that allow individuals to (1) construct a public or semi-public profile within a bounded system, (2) articulate a list of other users with whom they share a connection, and (3) view and traverse their list of connections and those made by others within the system.
>
> (p. 211)

Similarly, Kaplan and Haenlein (2010) provided an abbreviated definition of social media as "a group of Internet-based applications that build on the ideological and technological foundations of web 2.0, and that allow the creation and exchange of User Generated Content" (p. 61). The core assumptions regarding social media, therefore, are that (1) content is user generated, user controlled, and user shared, and (2) that this exchange takes place via a platform on an Internet site.

### Development of Social Media

The first social media platform that matched the above description began in 1997 with the launch of "Sixdegrees.com." Although this platform was unable to sustain business and closed in 2000, it was the catalyst for the start of LiveJournal, Ryze.com, Friendster, and many other similar services (Boyd & Ellison, 2007, pp. 214–216). In the years that followed, popular platforms such as Myspace, Facebook, Twitter, Instagram, and Snapchat have emerged. Each offers a unique flavor and approach to online community building.

In the last several years, social media technology has created new ways for individuals to interact and share information, such as snaps, vines, tweets, and posts. These new methods of interacting and sharing have altered the way that organizations or brands engage with publics. On a daily basis "billions of people create trillions of connections" through social media (Hansen, Shneiderman, & Smith, 2010, p. 3). Building conversations in social media with brand communities so that individual users are discussing the brand and its value is particularly effective because people are "more trusting of their own opinions and the opinions of their peers" as a result of the social media landscape (Hanna, Rohm, & Crittenden, 2011, p. 267). This focus on "bottom up," or user-generated conversations, as opposed to organizational dictated messaging, is reflected in the fact that publics have become active participants in the creation of brand messages, products, and causes. Users, therefore, are no longer merely consumers—they are invested publics who help shape the organizational culture and conversation. Mike DiLorenzo, the Director of Social Media Marketing and Strategy for the NHL, explains this change from static one-way communication to conversations, "Social networks aren't about Web sites. They're about experiences" (as quoted in Wyshynski, 2009).

It is the experience individuals have through social media that organizations need to focus on and understand in order to best connect with their social brand communities. To successfully interact with publics' social media experiences, Kietzmann, Hermkens, McCarthy, and Silvestre (2011) suggest looking at seven key parts: 1) identity, 2) conversations, 3) sharing, 4) presence, 5) relationships, 6) reputation, and 7) groups. These seven parts are directly tied to either individuals (identity and reputation), functions of social media (conversations and sharing), or formations of publics within the social media sphere (presence, relationships, and groups). Bringing these areas together in one brand community necessitates a strong commitment to the purpose of *social* media: relationships.

The truth is, discussions taking place about brands through social media highly influence the public perceptions of an organization or brand. In fact, today's media landscape makes the old adage "perception is reality" more true than ever before. The impact of perceptions via social media is why both intentionality and consistency are essential to reaching publics in a noisy world. No longer are brands solely concerned with those who are in physical proximity to the organization—rather, publics are diverse groups who actively engage in the online world, transcending the traditional geographic boundaries and time-zone limitations. Developing a platform in the digital environment requires the constant focus on publics who are non-geographically bound, creating dynamic engagement that initiates from the social community itself (Hyatt, 2012). This also makes Godin's (2008) concept of tribes foundational in understanding social media publics. Remember, Godin defines online publics, or tribes, as "a group of people connected to one another, connected to a leader, and connected to an idea. . . . A group needs only two things to be a tribe: a shared interest and a way to communicate" (pp. 1–2). The shared interest of groups is a core component of online communities. By finding a way to use social media platforms to reach these tribes, social media professionals enhance relationships and build credibility.

### Brand Communities

The term "brand community," originally used in relationship marketing theory (Webster, 1992; Morgan & Hunt, 1994), refers to the formation of a group of people in the digital world around a brand, organization, or cause. While some online communities are unified around topics or mutual interests, brand communities unite around the joint loyalty to an organization as their mutual interest. The main idea behind brand communities and management of digital relationships is that organizations need to sustain strong relationships, by utilizing technology, to meet publics' desires and needs in order to thrive (McKenna, 1991). It is within this effort that brand communities are sustained.

Muniz and O'Guinn (2001) describe a *brand community* as a "specialized non-geographically bound community, based on a structured set of social relationships among users of a brand" (p. 412). Again, relationships are a key component to any online community. Brand communities are made up not only of the relationship between publics and an organization or brand, but also between individuals who are affiliated with the brand community (McAlexander, Schouten, & Koenig, 2002). This means there is great value not only in the brand-to public relationship, but also in the relationships of various online community members with *each other* within a brand community. In the digital world, brands are able to develop a more robust "brand personality" that allows users to be more attached, engaged, and attracted to the brand (Aaker, 1997). Additionally, activities that take place within a brand community can generate value and energize the relationships around a brand (Schau, Muniz, & Arnould, 2009). Building commitment in social media communities is critical for relationships to thrive between brands and organizations.

### Commitment in Brand Communities

Previously, many organizations considered power and persuasion as key functions of interacting with publics (Webster, 1992; Morgan & Hunt,

1994). In today's networked world of social media, however, it is com-mitted relationships that are the key. Morgan and Hunt (1994) pointed out that "commitment and trust is central to successful relationship" building (p. 22). Every organization needs relationships to thrive and every relationship needs commitment and trust. They described commit-ment as an "ongoing relationship with another [that] is so important as to warrant maximum efforts at maintaining it" (p. 23). This is very similar to Moorman, Deshpandé, and Zaltman's (1993) definition that says, "Commitment to the relationship is defined as an enduring desire to maintain a valued relationship" (p. 316). The main idea, then, is that com-mitment in brand communities is the dedication of both the public and the brand to the value of and an intentional effort to maintain the relation-ship. The end-goal is not simply a transaction or a bottom-line financial gain. The goal of social media commitment is to sustain the valued rela-tionships developed in the brand community. Commitment, however, is dependent upon trust in an organization or brand, something that is more difficult due to the crisis of trust, which was previously discussed.

### Trust in Brand Communities

Organizational interaction with publics should be founded on trust, with the goal of creating mutually beneficial relationships (Morgan & Hunt, 1994). Gundlach and Murphy (1993) suggest that trust is the cornerstone of all long-term relationships between organizations and publics. Without trust, relationships erode and eventually disappear. Many additional stud-ies have found that trust is the primary determining factor for a long-term committed relationship with an organization or brand (Tax, Brown, & Chandrashekaran, 1998). This is why Berry (1996) says that "the inherent nature of services, coupled with abundant mistrust in America, posi-tions trust as perhaps the single most powerful relationship marketing tool available to a company" (p. 42). Trust is the crucial ingredient for relationships to last.

Essentially, trust is a belief that the organization or brand is reliable and has integrity (Morgan & Hunt, 1994, p. 23). Without that belief, relation-ships will fail. Social media has incredible potential to allow individual users to spread the message of an organization or brand, including the integrity and dependability of that brand, to a large number of people by simply sending a tweet, posting a photo, or uploading a video. The kind of power that individuals have through social media makes it all the more important for organizations or brands to build and *maintain* publics' trust. This trust directly enhances the organization's credibility. When this happens, the potential for effective social media engagement is established.

## Developing Engagement with Social Media Communities

Social media professionals have dedicated considerable resources to understanding how to develop engagement in social media communities. Organizations have, understandably, recognized the dynamic potential of one-to-one conversations that are made possible with publics via social media. For example, the way brands utilize mobile technology to intersect with social media and build relationships, or to ignite a widespread conversation around the organization or brand, is an area of significant focus as wearable technology grows in popularity (Alpert, 2012). Another example comes from Coyle, Smith, and Platt (2012), who examined how Twitter can play a key role in brand perception if a company uses Twitter to respond to consumer problems. They found that perceptions of the brand's trustworthiness increased when there were higher numbers of responses to problems. However, the response had to provide solutions, not simply empathetic comments. Briones, Kuch, Liu, and Jin (2011) explored the ways that the American Red Cross used social media to build relationships among publics such as volunteers and the media. They focused on two-way dialogue, the rapid release of information, and levels of control as components to the relationship-building process. And finally, though in no way exhaustively, another case study focused on the Gulf Coast oil spill. Strong relationships and credibility with publics have commonly been found to be key components of any disaster. Muralidharan, Dillistone, and Shin (2011) focused on these relationship components and credibility as they explored image restoration in the Gulf Coast oil spill through social media after the crisis.

Social media clearly has had a dynamic impact on organizations. As a result, the way social media professionals approach relationships, dialogue, and credibility has been the focus for many scholars and practitioners. In 2010, Smith proposed a "social model" of interaction for social media and public relations:

> In this social model, public relations-related activities are initiated by an online public, facilitated by the communication technology, and based on user interactivity (or the searching, retrieval, and distribution of information online). Whereas other online models consider the organization as source, in the dialogic web model (Kent et al., 2003), social public relations are based on user-initiation, and comprise three concepts: viral interaction, public-defined legitimacy, and social stake.
> (p. 333)

In other words, public relations in the social media world rests on the understanding that conversations, activities, and dialogue are driven by publics and not organizations. This is, as mentioned above, the core fabric of what drives and sustains social media communities.

Realizing that developing relationships through social media is pivotal to the growth of trust, relationships, and the perception of an organization's credibility, many professionals have proposed theories to support social media interaction. For example, Kerpen (2011) identified that listening, authenticity, transparency, and honesty are key factors in succeeding in the world of social media. Penenberg (2009) used the term "viral loop" to describe the value of customer dialogue, activity, and interaction on social sites. This loop is what Penenberg suggests businesses must develop not only to survive, but also to grow in the new digital world. This theory supports the overall development and historical nature of social media. In addition, Shih (2011) argued organizations must understand the "flattening effect" of social media which gives a voice to publics that might have been less vocal or less likely to engage in a relationship with the brand previously (p. 52). These studies, as well as many others, have found that just as with traditional media and with organizational spokespeople, social media has specific dimensions that enhance relationships between an organization and their publics. Transparency, two-way dialogue, expertise, and consistent interaction, for example, are factors of social media that directly impact the development of organizational relationships. Additionally, the way an organization develops their presence and the process they use to engage publics through social media is crucial. This includes determining which platforms are best for the organization's or brand's specific goals and audience, creating engaging content for the platforms and understanding how to correctly use and analyze data from the digital environment to further develop and enhance relationships.

### Social Media Tactics

Social media tactics tend to be what people most often think of when considering how brands can use social media. Thoughts such as "launch a contest" or "show a behind-the-scenes video" often quickly surface in conversations. That is because tactics can often be the most visible part of a campaign—they are what brands *do* in social media. The focus on tactics and the approach to using social media is an important area of study both for professionals and academics. Expertise in social media, however, is when brands recognize that tactics must be born out of specific strategies and objectives set by the organization. It is not a haphazard string of activities, but rather a specific engagement fueled by the research and design of the overall campaign.

One way brands develop tactics is by understanding how the culture of a social media community influences existing and new members in order to create engagement. Schau et al. (2009) found that, "If firms give consumers the opportunity to construct brand communities and the freedom to modify their products," the organization "should foster or sponsor social networking practices to build and sustain the community and to inspire further co-creation" (p. 41). In other words, the *ways* that online communities develop around an organization or brand can create patterns of interaction that contribute to publics' perceptions of the organization or brand. When this happens, not only does the brand gain value, but also value is given back to the publics. An example of this can be seen in Starbucks' #ProTip social media efforts. They regularly post tips and insight on how to order drinks or get the most out of a Starbucks experience using the hashtag "#ProTip". They have shared things like "#ProTip: Your local Starbucks can grind coffee for almost any brewer and filter. And it's free!" (Starbucks, 2015a) and "#ProTip: Add a pump of caramel to your #icedcoffee, sing, dance, have an awesome day" (Starbucks, 2015b). What happens with these types of tweets, however, is the real value. Members of the brand community add in their own tips, such as "#ProTip: When the sun is out, add a pump of vanilla syrup to your iced coffee. #CoffeePairings" (OCTA WISE, 2015). Starbucks as a brand created value by providing tips that the community wanted. This ignited conversations within the community, causing users to generate their own content and create value for other users by sharing useful tips. This creates value for the brand and for the community.

## The Need for More than Just Tactics

The growing focus on interactivity and customer care via social media may be why there are so many resources based on tactical approaches to maintaining a strong business presence in social media. A key ingredient in truly leveraging the power of social media for organizations, however, is to move beyond tactical understanding and into a paradigm of process. This was the point Jonathan Becher, CMO of international software provider SAP, made when he argued that social media is an *enabler,* but not the goal itself (Hong, 2014). Often, organizations are eager to jump into the social media world because it is what people expect, because there is the potential to create engagement, or simply because it is "the thing to do." The reality, however, is that social media should be approached more holistically, carefully considering the vision of the organization and the potential of social media to enhance their vision.

In the last decade, multiple resources have provided counsel on how social media can be capitalized on to build relationships, foster business ROI, and develop social communities. This focus on social communication is indicative of not only the opportunity available to organizations in the social world, but also the expectation from publics that businesses would utilize social media channels. For example, it has been found that while over 68% of organizations believe social media is an important communication channel (International Customer Management Institute, n.d.), nearly 70% of customers reaching out with complaints via Twitter never heard a response from the organization (Maritz Research & evolve24,

2011). In addition, over 87% of posts to brand pages on Facebook remain unanswered, with active, or the most engaged, pages answering only about 37% of brand engagement on their official profiles (Hutchinson, 2015). In addition, publics have a growing expectation that organizations will be highly interactive on social media. In fact, some studies suggest audiences expect a brand's response within 60 minutes (Gesenhues, 2013). This is increasing the pressure and expectation of communication brands must provide when in the social world. All in all, while the research supports the understanding that social media is important for relationships, there is a disconnect between this "best practice" and its practical outworking within the business world.

Strategic social media plans are much more than simply linking together tactics that other organizations have found effective. It is about the art and science of weaving together a brand community and an organization into a thriving, growing conversation in the social environment.

## Developing a Social Media Process

Some may think that the dynamic nature of social media is an environment that really cannot be mapped or placed into a planned process. After all, social media is about fluid conversations and relationships, not controlled propaganda or behavior. Because of this, it may seem contrary to the essence of social media to consider a model that would structure approaches to social media. The concerns regarding maintaining the flexibility and interactive nature of social media are real and important. However, while it is true that social media, by its very nature, is a vibrant environment with publics generating and driving the conversation, it does not follow that a model cannot be proposed by which professionals can strategically design campaigns for social media that support the overall organization's vision. Social media is no longer a new platform or an "arriving" way for organizations to communicate. It has arrived. What we see now in the social landscape, therefore, is a developing and maturing of frameworks for how organizations can fully engage with social media communities.

Social media's very fiber is that it is a dynamic conversation based on relationships. But the truth is, if an organization is not intentional about being present in those conversations, developing meaningful connections with key publics, it is very likely that the two-way dialogue and relationship will never thrive. Business is busy. Deadlines must be met. Without a dedicated focus on relationship within social media, the essence of the platform (relationships) gets altogether lost. It becomes an afterthought rather than the primary focus. When that happens, the value of social media to support the vision of the brand also diminishes.

In light of this, not only does a framework, or model, for social media campaigns allow professionals to better plan, prepare, and align their social media campaigns with the larger vision of the organizations for which they work, it also enables them to enhance the quality and value of social media within a business context. In the early days of social media, many perceived it to be of little bottom-line value in helping a business succeed. In recent years, however, organizations are requiring that social media professionals prove that the social initiatives help business objectives and relationships. A model that strategically outlines approaches to social media engagement by organizations empowers professionals to have a framework within which they can illustrate the value of social media for a brand. Research, design, engagement, and evaluation are all key components to a model for social media campaigns. Otherwise, social media activity becomes simply that: activity. It is not a uniquely crafted plan that has a strategic purpose. This is what Gary Vaynerchuk, Founder of VaynerMedia, highlighted when he said, "There is no ROI in anything if you don't learn how to use it" (Wong, 2014). We must know *how* to strategically leverage social media, not just the ways we can string together numerous tactics.

In addition to providing a framework to show the value of social media to an organization, a model also helps establish a framework within which brands can operate in ethical and transparent ways. Individuals in social communities expect personal, transparent, and genuine engagement. Sometimes, these expectations can seem to hinder the primary interest of organizations in social media: to succeed as a brand. There are limited time and resources, leaving brands to appear inauthentic or uninterested in two-way connections in social media. This tension is precisely why social media experts are needed! It is the ethical responsibility of a social media strategist to harmonize the commitment to an organization's vision, resources, and capabilities with the staunch dedication to authentic and trusted engagement within a brand community.

## Four-Step Process

The aim of this book is to explore a model for social media campaigns that provides a blueprint for professionals. While the reality of the social world dictates a certain level of fluidity and uncertainty, sometimes even chaos, when engaging in social media campaigns organizations that utilize a strategic process to develop an effective framework for campaigns have a stronger capacity to leverage the potential of social media.

This book proposes a four-step process, which should guide social media campaigns. While every campaign needs to have its own creative flair and original engagement, genuine expertise also recognizes that there are key elements, or steps, to social media campaigns. The four steps used to develop a structure in a way that professionals can purposefully design and engage with audiences around organizational objectives are: 1) Listening, 2) Strategic Design, 3) Implementation and Monitoring, and 4) Evaluation.

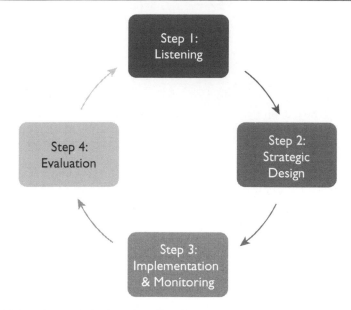

*Figure 1.3* The Social Media Four-Step Model

### Listening

The first step in any social media campaign is to listen. Think of this step as the *research* phase of the campaign process. In this phase, it is important to understand not only *how* to listen in the social media environment, but also to *what* one should be listening. The world of social media is littered with content. Expertise in social media, therefore, extends past one's ability to listen and into the ability to proficiently determine what to listen for and how to interpret that information into a meaningful plan for the organization.

### Strategic Design

After listening, the second step is to design the campaign. The goals, objectives, strategies, and tactics are all directly related to the information gathered in listening. During this step, professionals map out the entire social media campaign. The functionality and capabilities of certain platforms, as well as key business considerations that must go into every campaign, are taken into account. The strategic design and focus is then married in creative engagement pieces designed to ignite connection and conversations within brand communities. In addition, ethical foundations to guide strategic design are crucial to developing strong plans, ensuring that interaction is not dissected from a commitment to the quality and value of relationships.

## Implementation and Monitoring

Once a strategically designed campaign is created out of solid research, the next step is to implement the campaign. As with any marketing or public relations campaign, however, one cannot simply activate it and walk away. Professionals must fully monitor and engage with the campaign throughout its life-cycle. Within this step, it is vital that professionals interact and monitor so that campaign adjustments may be made, accountability to the value of social media within the organization is strong and, ultimately, the two-way dialogue nature of social media is protected. The process of monitoring and engaging relates directly to our social principle—social media is about relationships, not pre-programmed content that is pushed out without any live-time interaction.

## Evaluation

While analysis will naturally happen throughout the course of the campaign delivery (Step 3), it is important to clearly assess the effectiveness and growth opportunities of a campaign when it is complete. Evaluation requires measurement across social media platforms and a solid attribution strategy to be established for the value of social media in an overall digital campaign. The opportunity to evaluate a campaign is truly where social media professionals can highlight the value to the organization. It allows for the clear articulation of ROI and contribution to the organization's vision.

## KEY CONCEPT SNAPSHOT

1.  Today's brands operate in a society of deep mistrust for organizations. In order to address this, brands must build authentic, committed relationships based on trust.

2.  The historical development of social media as a communication platform is uniquely poised to address the issue of mistrust by facilitating two-way dialogue between organizations and key stakeholders. This communication is most powerful when purposefully designed yet placed in a framework that allows freedom to adapt and customize interaction.

3.  The Social Principle: the fluid nature of social media is designed for and sustained in *relationship* through two-way communication around topics of mutual interest that is user-generated, -created, and -driven.

4.  When organizations embrace the paradigm that social media is not simply a tool for publicity to plaster information in front of users, but rather a dynamic platform to foster two-way relationships in an

> unscripted environment, they are positioned to truly ignite their social communities.
>
> 5. Brands can use the four-step social media model to build dynamic campaigns that truly leverage the power of a social community: 1) research; 2) strategic design; 3) implementation and monitoring; and 4) evaluation.

## Suggested Reading

Baer, J. (2013). *Youtility: Why smart marketing is about help not hype.* New York: Portfolio/Penguin.

Brito, M. (2014). *Your brand, the next media company: How a social business strategy enables better content, smarter marketing and deeper customer relationships.* Indianapolis, IN: Que.

Schaefer, M. (2012). *Return on influence: The revolutionary power of Klout, social scoring, and influence marketing.* New York: McGraw-Hill.

## References

*Note*: All website URLs accessed on February 2, 2016.

Aaker, J. L. (1997). Dimensions of brand personality. *Journal of Marketing, 34*(3), 347–356.

Alpert, J. (2012). *The mobile marketing revolution: How your brand can have a one-to-one conversation with everyone.* New York: McGraw-Hill.

Baer, J. (2013). *Youtility: Why smart marketing is about help not hype.* New York: Portfolio/Penguin.

Bagozzi, R. P., & Dholakia, U. M. (2002). Intentional social action in virtual communities. *Journal of Interactive Marketing, 16*(2), 2–21.

Bennett, S. (2013, Jan. 4). 100 amazing social media statistics, facts and figures [Infographic]. *Adweek.* Retrieved from: www.adweek.com/socialtimes/100-social-media-stats/475180

Berry, L. (1996). Retailers with a future. *Marketing Management, 5*(Spring), 39–46.

Bhargava, R. (2012). *Likeonomics: The unexpected truth behind earning trust, influencing behavior, and inspiring action.* Hoboken, NJ: John Wiley & Sons.

Boyd, D., & Ellison, N. (2007). Social network sites: Definition, history and scholarship. *Journal of Computer-Mediated Communication, 13*(1), 210–230.

Briones, R. L., Kuch, B., Liu, B. F., & Jin, Y. (2011). Keeping up with the digital age: How the American Red Cross uses social media to build relationships. *Public Relations Review, 37*(1), 37–43.

Brito, M. (2014). *Your brand, the next media company: How a social business strategy enables better content, smarter marketing, and deeper customer relationships.* Indianapolis, IN: Que.

Coyle, J. R., Smith T., & Platt, G. (2012). I'm here to help: How companies microblog responses to consumer problems influence brand perceptions. *Journal of Research in Interactive Marketing, 6*(1), 27–41.

Gesenhues, A. (2013, Oct. 30). Study: 72% of consumers expect brands to respond within an hour to complaints posted on Twitter. *Marketing Land*. Retrieved from: http://marketingland.com/study-72-of-consumers-expect-brands-to-respond-within-an-hour-to-complaints-posted-on-twitter-63496

Godin, S. (2008). *Tribes: We need you to lead us*. New York: Portfolio.

Gundlach, G., & Murphy, P. (1993). Ethical and legal foundations of relational marketing exchanges. *Journal of Marketing, 57*(4), 35–46.

Hanna, R., Rohm, A., & Crittenden, V. (2011). We're all connected: The power of the social media ecosystem. *Business Horizons, 54*(3), 265–273.

Hansen, D., Shneiderman, B., & Smith, M. A. (2010). *Analyzing social media networks with nodeXL: Insights from a connected world*. Amsterdam/Boston: M. Kaufmann.

Hong, P. (2014, Sept. 8). SAP's CMO shares 7 ways brands can create powerful connections. *Momentology*. Retrieved from: www.momentology.com/302-saps-cmo-shares-7-ways-brands-can-create-powerful-connections/

Hutchinson, A. (2015, June 17). 87% of user posts on Facebook pages ignored [Report], *Social Media Today*. Retrieved from: www.socialmediatoday.com/social-business/adhutchinson/2015-06-17/87-user-posts-facebook-pages-ignored-report?utm_content=16416336&utm_medium=social&utm_source=googleplus

Hyatt, M. (2012). *Platform: Get noticed in a noisy world*. Nashville, TN: Thomas Nelson.

International Customer Management Institute (n.d.). *Social customer care study*. Retrieved from: www.five9.com/social-customer-care-infographic

Kaplan, A. M., & Haenlein, M. (2010). Users of the world, unite! The challenges and opportunities of social media. *Business Horizons, 53*(1), 59–68.

Kerpen, D. (2011). *Likeable social media: How to delight your customers, create an irresistible brand, and be generally amazing on Facebook (& other social networks)*. New York: McGraw-Hill.

Kietzmann, J. H., Hermkens, K., McCarthy, I. P., & Silvestre, B. S. (2011). Social media? Get serious! Understanding the functional building blocks of social media. *Business Horizons, 54*(3), 241–251.

Maritz Research & evolve24 (2011). *Twitter study*. Retrieved from: www.maritzresearch.com/~/media/Files/MaritzResearch/e24/ExecutiveSummaryTwitterPoll.ashx

McAlexander, J. H., Schouten, J. W., & Koenig, H. F. (2002). Building brand community. *Journal of Marketing, 66*(1), 38–54.

McKenna, R. (1991). Marketing is everything. *Harvard Business Review, 69*(1), 65–79.

Moorman, C., Deshpandé, R., & Zaltman, G. (1993). Factors affecting trust in market research relationships. *Journal of Marketing, 57*(1), 81–101.

Morgan, R. M., & Hunt, S. D. (1994). The commitment trust theory of relationships marketing. *Journal of Marketing, 58*, 20–38.

Muniz, A. M., & O'Guinn, T. C. (2001). Brand community. *Journal of Consumer Research, 27*(4), 412–432.

Muralidharan, S., Dillistone, K., & Shin, J. (2011). The Gulf Coast oil spill: Extending the theory of image restoration discourse to the realm of social media and beyond petroleum. *Public Relations Review, 37*(3), 226–232.

OCTAWISE. (OCTA WISE). (2015, May 29). #ProTip: When the sun is out, add a pump of vanilla syrup to your iced coffee. #CoffeePairings [Tweet]. Retrieved from: https://twitter.com/octawise/status/604201327523061760

Penenberg, A. (2009). *Viral loop: From Facebook to Twitter, how today's smartest businesses grow themselves*. New York: Hyperion.

Rheingold, H. (2000). *The virtual community: Homesteading on the electronic frontier*. Cambridge, MA: MIT Press.

Ridings, C. M., & Gefen, D. (2004). Virtual community attraction: Why young people hang out online. *Journal of Computer-Mediated Communication, 10*(1), 1–42.

Schau, H. J., Muniz, A. M., & Arnould, E. (2009). How brand community practices create value. *Journal of Marketing, 73*(5), 30–51.

Shih, C. (2011). *The Facebook era: Tapping online social networks to market, sell, and innovate*. Upper Saddle River, NJ: Prentice Hall.

Smith, B.G. (2010). Socially distributing public relations: Twitter, Haiti, and interactivity in social media. *Public Relations Review, 36*(4), 329–335.

Starbucks [Starbucks Coffee]. (2015a, April 22). #ProTip: Your local Starbucks can grind coffee for almost any brewer and filter. And it's free! [Tweet]. Retrieved from: https://twitter.com/starbucks/status/590947495053631488

Starbucks [Starbucks Coffee]. (2015b, May 26). #ProTip: Add a pump of caramel to your #icedcoffee, sing, dance, have an awesome day [Tweet]. Retrieved from: https://twitter.com/starbucks/status/603183820888625154

Tax, S., Brown, S. W., & Chandrashekaran, M. (1998). Customer evaluation of service complaint experiences: Implications for relationship marketing. *Journal of Marketing, 62*(2), 60–76.

Webster, F. E. (1992). The changing role of marketing in corporations. *Journal of Marketing, 56*(4), 1–17.

Wong, K. (2014, May 13). What is the value of social media engagement? *Forbes*. Retrieved from: www.forbes.com/sites/kylewong/2014/05/13/what-is-the-value-of-social-media-engagement/

Wyshynski, G. (2009, Oct. 29). Inside NHL's social media innovations, growing pains. *Yahoo Sports*. Retrieved from: http://sports.yahoo.com/nhl/blog/puck_daddy/post/Inside-the-NHL-s-social-media-innovations-growi?urn=nhl,199092

# Chapter 2

# Step 1: Listening

## Developing Research, Discovering Data, and Applying Meaning

Social media expertise stems from informed decisions leading to strategic design. The ability for a social media professional to discover needed information, determine how to understand the context of that data and provide meaningful application into a social media campaign is paramount.

The first step in developing a social media strategic campaign is to *listen*. This *listening*, or formative research, phase is where social media strategists collect data required to make informed decisions that will form the foundation for a campaign. There are two primary areas involved in the listening stage: 1) foundational background, and 2) social landscape. Both will be addressed within this chapter.

### Foundational Background

In preparing to craft a social media campaign that truly enhances an organization's goals, it is vital to have a strong understanding of the organization itself. This is because when the vision of the organization is separated from social engagement, the brand will be significantly limiting the full potential and influence social media provides as a relationship-building platform. Social media is an extension of communication from the organization toward the publics—it is rooted in a commitment to relationships and dialogue. To segment social media away from the rest of the organization, making it a tool that gets used each time a brand wants to publicize information, reveals a deep misunderstanding about the purpose of *social* media. Thus, a truly powerful approach to social media requires brands to connect the vision of the organization into the social media efforts. An organization's social media strategy, therefore, should be born out of the organization's mission and values. If an organization leverages the social media well, it can be a natural extension of the organization into the social media world, uniquely planned to support the brand's needs.

| Foundational Background | | | |
|---|---|---|---|
| **Mission Statements** | **Organizational Structure** | **Communication Audit** | **Policies & Procedures** |
| • Social strategists recognize that each campaign, strategy, and tactic in social media should relate to the brand's vision. Informed social media engagement relates to the core essence, or mission statement, of the brand. | • Strategists use data from the organizational structure research to determine the level of support for social media integration into the core processes of a brand, as well as the appropriate type of social media team to create in order to help a brand thrive in the social environment. | • Data from communication audits display the tapestry of ways that key publics are being communicated with, informing key elements of message structure and timing within a campaign's design. | • Employee handbooks, brand guides, crises response plans, market research, and SEO & Web Analytic reports all provide key information into the ways that an organization communicates its values and engages with key stakeholders. Applying this information to a campaign design is critical to ensuring that the social initiatives are consistent with the brand's business model and values. |

*Figure 2.1* Foundational Background for Research

## Mission Statement

Before developing a plan to build relationships and engage in the communities that are connected to the business, it is crucial to first understand why the organization exists. The first step, therefore, in formative research is to review the brand's mission or vision statement, value commitments, and even strategic plans. These are helpful to analyze and apply to the social media process as it will provide the direction for the social media strategy. After understanding the purpose of the organization, it is also important to evaluate how the organization functions in order to truly leverage the power of social media within the brand's structure.

**Key Data Application:** Social strategists recognize that each campaign, strategy, and tactic in social media should relate to the brand's vision. Informed social media engagement relates to the core essence, or mission statement, of the brand.

## Organizational Structure

After developing a solid understanding of what the organization is about and what differentiates them from any other business, the next step is to identify the structure of the organization. When it is time to develop key messaging and communication maps that include all relevant participants from the organization, knowledge of how management is set up, how departments are structured within the organization, and who is responsible for each component will be important. Be sure to pay special attention to the marketing, public relations, communication, and IT department structure. All of these departments tend to be required in developing an effective and integrated social media campaign.

## Discovering Support for Social Media Team Structure

Part of what occurs during the listening phase of a social media campaign is the process of gathering information on what kind of social media team or structure would thrive within the organization. To gather the best information possible on what kind of social team structure will work, it is important to look at: leadership, key players, and required skills.

### LEADERSHIP

Organizations that truly desire to engage the powerful potential of social media to build key relationships must recognize that it starts with the top of the organization. It is presidents and CEOs that need to lead the organization into a social culture. Jim Claussen (2015), Senior Strategy Manager for Social Business at IBM, identifies the kind of leaders that organizations need today as "blue unicorns." He defines blue unicorns as "the rare leaders who are transforming their leadership for today's connected social economy" (para. 3). While some brands may argue that having leadership that is social is not a necessity, Ted Coiné and Mark Babbitt (2014) suggest that in the future, "An engaging presence on social media will not just be 'nice to have,' it will be considered a leadership competency" (p. 128). In other words, brands need top leadership to value social media.

As part of the organizational structure research on leadership, discover whether the top leader(s) in the organization are active on any social media accounts and review what level of engagement they seem to take with social media communication. In addition, take time to meet with the leadership to understand their view of the role and value of social media in the life of the brand and their personal dedication (or hesitation) to be involved in social communication. One important concept to get a pulse on is whether or not top leadership is willing and ready to maintain their own social media activity. While some leadership seems to express commitment to social media by being willing to allow a social media team to run their personal social media presence, this approach to social media engagement for leadership is not advisable. Coiné and Babbitt (2014) highlight this kind of approach as an "insincere social leader," likening it to the absurd idea of sending a proxy to a business dinner, dressed up like the CEO, speaking like the CEO, and introducing himself or herself as the CEO, but not actually being the CEO (p. 128). A brand leader would never embrace that kind of inauthentic communication with publics in face-to-face settings. It should not be acceptable in social media either.

KEY PLAYERS

The social media team or department of an organization will likely be divided into two groups. The first group is what Michael Brito (2014) called the "Social Business Center of Excellence (CoE)" (p. 60). The people who compose the CoE for an organization need to be individuals who have leadership influence, the ability to apply action to organizational behaviors, and are deeply committed to the integration of social media as part of organizational life. The CoE needs to be composed of individuals who play a leadership role in the organization's business behaviors and communication. For example, key people to include would be the head of marketing, the director of PR, the top research analysts, the manager of information technologies, and the social media director. The CoE's role is to envision the potential for complete social integration within the organization, understanding the power of two-way dialogue throughout the life-blood of a brand: from employee orientation to customer interaction, from leadership communication to the brand ambassador program. Instead of simply seeing social media as a tack-on to communication efforts, or a secret weapon to drive sales, the CoE is composed of social visionaries that lead the way for an organization to integrate the power of two-way dialogue in real-time communication via social media into core practices of an organization. The goal of the CoE is to succeed

> at changing organizational behavior—the way it thinks, communicates, and markets to customers. In doing so, the members must adapt and change their own behavior at the same time. They must become change agents if they truly want to see the transformation come to fruition.
> (p. 60)

To determine the best people to be on a CoE, it is crucial that research is done to understand which departments within an organization carry out certain responsibilities (such as technology roll-outs, communication with clients, communication with customers, employee relations, etc.). Then, identify which individuals within those departments have the capacity, authority, and vision to be part of the CoE. The second group is the individuals who are tasked with maintaining and engaging the organization's social media platforms. In the research phase of a social media campaign it is important to identify whether the organization has resources for a team to be employed, the number of positions available, and the skills or qualifications that are needed. In order to identify what kind(s) of people are needed on a social media team, identifying key skills is necessary.

## SKILLS

It is crucial to determine what skills may already be available for the team, due to existing staff or structures, what skills may be lacking, and what structure of a team might work for the given organization's long-term approach to social engagement. In describing needed skills/staff members for real-time marketing campaigns in social media, Chris Kerns (2014) suggests the following areas: program lead, creative lead, copy lead, social lead, and analysts (pp. 158–160). While real-time responses will be covered later, this structure is a helpful starting point in identifying key areas that a social team needs. The reality is that some organizations may have the resources to employ a team of social media pros, letting incredible expertise and specialization be part of each job description. Other organizations may be lucky if they have one or two people working on social media. Whether it is a team of 100 or a team of one, strong social media teams need the following skills.

*Leader*   Each social media team needs a leader. Whether they are called the program lead, social media director, or some other title, the key responsibilities of this individual are to lead the strategy for the social media engagement on behalf of the organization, to advocate for social integration across the brand, and to guide the other members on the social team. People who fill this role need key competencies not only in social media but also in business acumen. This person should have strategic foresight, be able to skillfully articulate the value and need for social media among the CoE and with upper management, and have a strong grasp of team-dynamics and people skills. It is their job to develop, lead, and manage the social media strategy and also to encourage the individuals on the social team to develop as professionals.

*Word Artisans*   Social media should be engaging, punchy, and to-the-point. Word artisans seem to effortlessly engage in 140 characters but can also weave together a beautiful post to accompany an infographic on Facebook. Grammar, style, and vocabulary are core to this skill. Word artisans are the kind of people that you could listen to all day simply because the *way* they communicate is unique, it catches your ear (or eye), and takes a new approach even if talking about a common topic. In the research phase, take time to identify who the word artisan would be for social media campaigns. If there is not a set position in social media, is there someone on the team who is a natural with words? Perhaps the communication or marketing department has an individual who would take on the responsibility of helping craft messages.

*Creative Gurus*    Visual engagement is on the rise in social media. Instagram, Snapchat, and Vine—these are all media that rely solely on the power of an image. Most likely more visually based platforms are on the horizon and poised to be the most prominent social media platforms available. Having a creative guru on the team, therefore, is a must. Sometimes the creative guru and word artisan are one and the same—and other times, someone who is fantastic with the written word seems to struggle with finding that perfect image (or filter). As with the word artisan, be resourceful in identifying who would be a potential fit for this necessary position on the social media team. Additionally, do research on apps, tools, and subscriptions that are available to help the social team succeed. The marketing or PR department may already have a subscription to an image library that is available for use, or perhaps the organization has other processes to develop creative pieces across the brand. Be sure to have done enough research to identify each resource available to help the creative guru succeed.

*Social Designer*    The social lead is relied upon to marry the power of a post with the potential of a platform. They are tasked with identifying the right type of content and topic with the right platform, working closely with the other members of the team to strategize creative ways to capitalize on certain social media functions (such as a story versus a snap in Snapchat, or the reason one might choose to run a Twitter chat or provide a Facebook giveaway). On smaller teams, this skillset is placed with the social media director, as they formulate the overall strategy and help guide the other members of the team toward success.

*Data Analyst*    This will be discussed in greater detail later, but each social media team needs an analyst. The ability to gather data, apply that information, and adjust social media initiatives is a must in today's social world. As with other skills that the team needs, the data pro may be combined with some other skills into one job description. Alternatively, the data might come from a variety of other places such as working closely with marketing research or the website analyst to help interpret the data. Whatever model best serves the size of organization, regular review and application of data is crucial.

Having identified what skills, positions, and people should be part of a social media campaign, the next area to collect data on is the overall communication from the organization.

**Key Data Application:** Strategists use data from the organizational structure research to determine the level of support for social media integration into the core processes of a brand, as well as the appropriate type of social media team to create in order to help a brand thrive in the social environment.

## Communication Audit

Social media communication should harmonize with other communication platforms and initiatives from the organization. A *communication audit* is a comprehensive analysis of all information being communicated by the brand and a review of the intended audience and desired outcome expected from sharing that information. Create a list that identifies all the ways that the public is communicated with by the organization. Be sure to classify the type of communication platform (such as a newsletter, media relations efforts, community events, etc.), the intended audience (employees, consumers, donors, etc.), the frequency of the communication (such as how often the website is updated, when consumer emails are sent, or the timing of speeches by the CEO), and the person or department responsible for developing and managing the specific communication piece. The next step in formative research is to understand any policies that guide organizational activities or procedures developed to structure the communication process.

**Key Data Application:** Data from communication audits display the tapestry of ways that key publics are being communicated with, informing key elements of message structure and timing within a campaign's design.

## Policies and Procedures

Having identified the core vision for the organization, how it is structured and how it communicates to all publics, it is also helpful to understand any existing policies or procedures that will impact the social media campaign design.

### Employee Handbook

Reading through the employee handbook for the organization will provide a lot of insight into the culture of the organization. It should also clarify expectations of employees, responsibilities for employees and, potentially, any information that already exists about how employees are trained on interacting via social media. Ideally, social media training will be part of every new employee training seminar as well as incorporated into a regular rotation for existing employee training to make sure everyone is aware of policies and guidelines. This will be discussed in greater detail in Chapter 3.

**Key Data Application:** The way in which employees are introduced, trained, and encouraged to share their stories on social media directly influences the brand's voice and influence in social media. Understanding the role of employees in a social media brand's voice provides key insights into designing campaign tactics.

## Brand Guide

The marketing or public relations department for the organization will likely have this on hand. It will include all the guidelines for colors and font choices with the brand logo, instructions on messaging or positioning, and information on the brand persona. Understanding the brand persona for the organization is crucial in social media. Moving forward with designing a social media campaign, it is important to ensure that the voice and personality that is portrayed in social media reflects the organization in a unified manner, consistent with other communication pieces. People should not experience one kind of organization if they came by the offices and another when they visit the social media profiles. By being thoroughly familiar with the brand guidelines, there will be a higher likelihood of success in unifying the brand persona both in social media and in other communication outlets. A more detailed process to develop and design specific communication messages for social media in line with the brand persona is discussed in Chapter 3.

**Key Data Application:** Social media is one way in which a brand communicates, not the *only* way. Familiarity with the brand's requirements and voice allows social media initiatives to enhance branding and connection rather than creating a division between the brand's presence on social media and its presentation in other platforms.

## Crisis Response Plan

It is important that a social media strategist has access to the organizational crisis response plan. Social media during a crisis needs to fully align with the larger crisis response of the organization. It may be that the organization has already identified the role and functions social media will fulfill in a crisis, but if that is not the case, it is important for the social media team to be aware of the entire crisis plan so a fully integrated social media crisis response document can be developed. The process to develop and design a crisis response is explained in Chapter 3.

**Key Data Application:** Every organization will face crises and social media will play a key role. Crisis plans allow social media teams to be prepared and equipped to engage in a crisis, rather than forcing them to respond in the moment, which often leads to increased problems.

## Market Research

Reach out to the marketing department to get the latest market research for the organization. This will identify key audiences that should be considered in social media. While it may be that not all of the audiences identified in the market research apply specifically to social media, the strategic insight gained from reviewing the market research for an organization will save a lot of time in developing a social media campaign that aligns with the overall communication efforts of an organization.

Additionally, within the market research report, or potentially housed in another more specific report by the marketing department, specific return on investment (ROI) metrics may be identified for types of behaviors. For example, the marketing department should have a report that clarifies what the value of a name for someone who signs up for a newsletter is for the brand, the value assigned to leads generated for certain types of sales, or the life-time value of a new donor. Whatever the organization is measuring and assigning value to, be sure to have a full list and details on the exact ROI numbers. These metrics are crucial in the next stage (designing a strategic plan) as it allows the social media strategist to understand any tangible, bottom-line goals that can be linked to social media activity.

**Key Data Application:** The marketing team will have a wealth of information on key publics. While not all of it will be applicable, social strategists glean key points from these reports and apply them to the publics who are active on social media in order to create a more effective campaign design.

### Search Engine Optimization and Website Analytic Reports

While it may seem like search engine optimization (SEO) and website analytic reports are not areas in which social media professionals must be versed, the reality is that SEO is highly influenced by social media. In addition, social media optimization is a growing focus within the industry as platform algorithms are having a greater influence on social media reach. There is a wealth of information available in both the SEO and the analytic reports. For example, in the SEO report, it is possible to identify the keywords and phrases that drive the most traffic and the top pages that are optimized on the website. These findings are significant to the organization and so allow a social strategist to understand keywords that are important to integrate into social media and potential webpages that are most effective to link to from social media. Even if in-depth analytics have not been set up, a basic analytics report can provide insight on the demographics of your online audience, typical actions (also known as conversions) such as purchases or sign-ups, the typical online path people follow when exploring the website, and social media traffic sources. This is just a small portion of what is available in these reports. In order to effectively create a strong listening strategy and develop a strategic campaign that relates to the larger goals of the organization, be sure that a thorough review of both documents is completed in the formative research phase as it provides a strong platform to move forward with social media design. After gathering all the information available on the organization's background and processes, it is now time to develop formative research within a social media context.

Key Data Application: The SEO and website analytic reports provide key details regarding the online behaviors of audiences. Social strategists apply this information to the unique needs of social media brand communities in order to design engaging and effective digital tactics.

## Social Landscape

Having completed the foundational research, it is now possible to effectively survey the social landscape in the context of its application to an organization. In this phase of the listening (research) stage, the goal is to identify what conversations are taking place on social media that may be relevant to the brand, who is having those conversations, and ways that the organization might engage with that dialogue. It is important to remember that even in listening, which can often seem removed and objective rather than relational and engaged, social media is about humanizing communication. Listening, then, is not cold and mechanized but rather about understanding and seeing the people that are important to the brand. Dave Kerpen (2011, p. 24) advocates for the power of social listening by saying,

> Listening is the single most important skill in social media, and one that's easy to forget once you get started with all of the sexier, more exciting things you can do. So whatever you do, once you start, never stop listening.

### Key Listening Phrases

The first step for this stage is to identify all the categories to listen to within social media. Some people identify these as "keywords." A keyword is more than simply a single word, however. It can be an entire phrase. The idea is to write out what words or phrases someone in social media may be using to discuss topics that pertain to the organization or brand. Keywords will fall into two categories: specific and generic. The SEO report gathered earlier will likely have a list of keywords already used by the organization. This can be very useful in creating a social media list as it will save time and a great deal of research. Identify specific words to search for that will open up opportunities to join in on social conversations. In addition, keywords are concepts that people type into a search bar within social media in order to find conversations related to things they care about. When making a keyword list, it is important to consider not only what the organization thinks are important conversations, but also what social media users would think of when trying to reach information available from your organization. Remember, organizations are not making a conversation on social media—they are *joining* the conversation. This means they must be able to find out where the conversation is

## Social Landscape

| Key Listening Phrases | Conversation Platforms | Brand Community Dialogue | Influencers | Competition |
|---|---|---|---|---|
| • The key listening phrase list will provide valuable data as to what topics are most meaningful and the many types of words that people use when joining these conversations. When it comes the time to craft messaging, this information informs content design. | • Key listening phrases revealed what conversations are taking place and the Conversation Platform research reveals where those conversations are happening. This data helps in crafting the appropriate type of content for the right kind of platform in a campaign. | • Audience analysis, content evaluation, community engagement, and brand dialogue provide key insights into the way two-way interaction is driven and sustained within a brand community. This information should be applied when crafting campaign messaging in order to ensure robust engagement is created in campaign tactics. | • Within each brand community, there are key individuals who drive conversations forward and truly ignite connection. These influencers should be identified and specifically encouraged to participate within a campaign. | • Competition analysis allows brands to identify what type of content is generally the most effective across an industry, to identify engaging profile creation, and ultimately to evaluate the brand's Share of Voice and sentiment score within the social landscape. This information can then be used to inform specific tactical creation within a campaign as well as serving as a benchmark to evaluate the success of campaign messaging. |

*Figure 2.2* Social Landscape Research

taking place and who is participating. This is where specific and generic keywords come into play.

## Specific

Specific keywords are those words or phrases that are unique to the organization. They may include the names of key people, such as the president or CEO, the name of a specific product or service, or the tagline or slogan for the company. If the brand has launched any specific public relations campaigns or marketing initiatives, it is also useful to include those phrases or keywords within this list. Keep track of every keyword within a document to apply to later strategy.

## Generic

Keywords or phrases that fall into the generic category are a goldmine for many brands. However, organizations often forget to create a generic keyword list and only focus on those specific terms that apply only to the brand. Thus, they miss out on some very relevant and vibrant social conversations. When developing a generic list, identify categories that publics connected to the organization deeply care about. For example, a coffee company could identify generic keywords like "coffee brewing," "coffee beans," and "coffee grains." While these are not specific to any individual coffee brand, people who drink coffee would likely engage with those topics.

The goal is to identify what online communities care about and want to be discussing. The brand is joining a conversation with people who have a mutual interest. What brought the social media community that the brand cares about together into a virtual tribe and provides a commonality that connects? When those areas are identified, the generic keywords are developed. Think through words and phrases that relate to the industry, services, products, and vision.

**Key Data Application:** The key listening phrase list will provide valuable data as to what topics are most meaningful and the many types of words that people use when joining these conversations. When it comes the time to craft messaging, this information informs content design.

## Conversations on Platforms

Having developed a robust list of what phrases and words are relevant to the organization within the social media landscape, it is now time to find out *where* these conversations are taking place. There are a number of tools that are available to do this. Many may choose to listen to platforms by using the search functions available on each social media site. For example, it is possible to use the advanced search on Twitter to find specific conversations. Social strategists may also choose to do a similar search in Facebook, narrowing the conversation by top posts or people or even photos. Carefully analyze the data to ensure that the data is not simply a review of information from people that the organization is somehow connected to through social media (people within the brand's likes, friends, followers, etc.). Do a public, or "all user," search.

Many people prefer to use tools that aggregate data from several platforms to ensure a more robust analysis and save time. Hootsuite is one of the leading platforms for this type of research. Several other platforms (at the time of this book's writing) include Social Mention, Topsy, and TweetDeck. The value of having a place that analyzes multiple social channels at once is to not only identify the genres of conversations taking place on social media with specific keywords, but also what the quality of the conversation is, who is participating, and how it compares to other platforms in an expedited fashion. The goal is to use this real-time data to make informed decisions in building a strategic campaign.

Using these tools, go through all the relevant conversations that are taking place on the social platform. By adding a column next to each of the keywords previously identified, keep a list of which platforms have the largest conversation around a given topic or keyword. For example, it could be that on Twitter, people are more interested in certain topics than on Facebook. This data can provide key insights that can help in the development of a stronger message map. In addition to the platforms and conversations taking place, identify who participates in the conversations and who has the largest impact when they interact. These people are known as influencers and are key individuals to connect and interact with throughout social media initiatives. Finally, be sure to note the tone

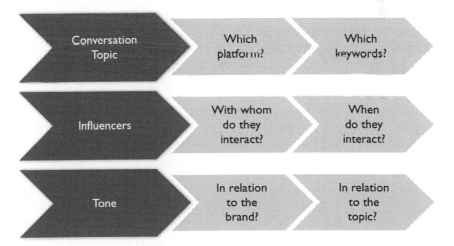

*Figure 2.3* The Social Conversation Check-List

of the conversations. People may have a positive tone, generally, when talking about a specific brand name but a negative tone with some of the generic topics. Again, this will come in handy in developing messaging for social media.

**Key Data Application:** Key listening phrases revealed *what* conversations are taking place and the Conversation Platform research reveals *where* those conversations are happening. This data helps in crafting the appropriate type of content for the right kind of platform in a campaign.

### Brand Community Dialogue

Understanding what conversations are taking place and who is participating in the general social media landscape, it is time to examine the online communities for the brand. There are several steps to take when evaluating the climate of social media communities.

**Key Data Application:** Audience analysis, content evaluation, community engagement, and brand dialogue provide key insights into the way two-way interaction is driven and sustained within a brand community. This information should be applied when crafting campaign messaging in order to ensure robust engagement is created in campaign tactics.

#### Audience Analysis

The very first place to begin is to understand who is involved in the organization's social media communities. In an *audience analysis,* brands create a profile of key publics by providing basic demographic and behavioral information that helps brands to identify the appropriate platforms and methods for engagement. The previous reports from the marketing department on market research will be helpful with this step. That report will detail the general audiences for the organization, usually identifying the primary and secondary audiences for the brand. In addition, the reports should provide general information about key audiences, including details such as demographics, which communication channels are most effective for reaching specific audiences, and the behavioral analysis of the audience.

It is also helpful to review the website analytics report that should be able to identify which social media sites are sending visitors to the organization's website, what those visitors are doing once they reach the website, whether they complete an action that is valuable to an organization (which is a concept known as "converting individuals" (sign up for a newsletter, purchase a product, etc.)), and any other online trends that are monitored by the organization. All of this information should be compiled to provide a complete analysis of the audiences on social media.

**Key Data Application:** Having reviewed the general audience research for the organization, compare those findings and data with the current social media community in order to understand what values and content are most meaningful for the social media community. There are several ways to analyze a social media audience, including:

- Comparing the geographic region of the various platforms' online communities to the geographic regions of the general audience analysis from the organization. Next, dive deeper into the marketing analysis regarding behaviors and communication preferences for individuals from those various regions identified as active in social media to apply that information into message design within the campaign.
- Analyze the demographics such as age and gender from the website analytic report for all users who arrive at the website from social media platforms. Determine the typical needs of those users (which pages they were going to, what content was available), and the behaviors of those users (did they convert, did they stay on the page, did they share any content). This information will pinpoint some of the key values for the brand's social media community and how those can be highlighted within a campaign.
- Review the user paths, or the order of pages that users view on a website, among the individuals coming to the website from social media channels. Do they seem interested in specific sections of the website? If so, that may identify specific information needs of the social media audience. Do they seem to jump page to page rather quickly, but eventually take an action? If so, that may indicate that social media posts prepared them in advance to convert and the users are more interested in a behavioral objective once they reach the website.

It is important to remember that while the detailed analysis of the general audience for the organization through marketing will provide analysis of online community behavior, a social strategist's ability to integrate that understanding of the typical online behaviors with the brand's social media community will be crucial. The social media community will be unique. *Through audience analysis, identify which people from the general audience of the organization are using social media, what they are using it for, and what actions or behaviors they take as a result of that interaction.*

## Content

The next area to review is the kind of content that has previously been posted within the social media channels. Develop an in-depth understanding of each platform. Review whether there is a rhythm to the split between original content in posts, curated content, whether posts are from partner organizations, and how often content is discussing topics other than the brand itself. Identify how frequently content is posted and whether there seem to be specific genres that are typical on the platform. Keep notes, as this will clarify previous social media engagement approaches that will help inform future action.

**Key Data Application:** Social media campaign development needs a historical understanding of how information was shared previously with the brand community. Each platform's historical content and data distribution plan needs to be analyzed in order to effectively design a content calendar that resonates with the brand community.

---

## EXPERT INSIGHT

*Stephen Waddington*

**What do you think is one hallmark competency social media professionals need to succeed?**

Professionals need to be actively engaged in using social forms of media. A basic understanding of theory is important but there is no better way of understanding how content, conversations, and network work.

**What is the value, if any, of listening within social media before launching into a campaign?**

It is absolutely critical. Social media activity should start with listening. Whatever your market, product, or service you'll almost certainly find relevant conversations taking place around the social web. These will provide useful information for your organization.

**Are there areas you've identified as the bread-and-butter for brands to focus in on when doing research before a campaign?**

I disagree with this point. Start with Google. There is then a huge third-party market of tools that you can use as the entry point to understand where the conversations relevant to your organization are taking place and what people are talking about.

**Do you have any tips or strategies for how social media professionals should sort through the data gathered in social media listening in order to make meaningful application to campaigns?**

Surface the key issue relevant to your organization, its market, products, and services. Rank these by topic pulling out the top three to five issues. Then for each topic determine how your organization

---

would be able to add value to the conversation. These are the areas that you should focus on in developing content.

**How can brands identify which influencers are most important for their social media efforts?**

A network typically consists of content creators (1%), curators or editors that share content (9%), and consumers (90%). There's a burgeoning third-party tool market to help map and understand the make-up of networks and identify creators, curators, and editors. Typically individuals are ranked for context, reach, and resonance.

**What's something that is often overlooked but could provide a lot of value for brands within the listening phase of social media?**

There's often a lack of rigor to planning within public relations. Practitioners jump directly to a network without properly inter-rogating whether it is the most appropriate form of media for their public. My recommendation is always to follow a formal planning process.

**Is there some example of the power of listening within social media that you've experienced as a professional?**

There are lots of excellent case studies but my personal favorite is the Harry Potter franchise. Listening by W20 Group identified 43 influencers responsible for conversation and content sharing online. Its work now focuses on this community.

**Connect with Stephen:** @wadds | https://uk.linkedin.com/in/stephenwaddington

*Stephen Waddington is the Chief Engagement Officer at Ketchum and a Visiting Professor at the University of Newcastle*

## Community Engagement

Since the entire point of social media is to be *social*, evaluate whether the brand community is interacting with the content in any way. Keep in mind: different types of engagement carry different "value" within the social world. For example, when someone likes a photo on Instagram, it is a fairly easy action to take and, therefore, carries less weight or value. When someone comments, however, it takes a little bit more work on his or her part and, therefore, carries more weight. Actions that take more work on behalf of a brand community in social media tend to indicate a deeper commitment or passion to the topic, brand, or conversation. These actions by community members influence algorithms within many social media platforms and impact whether content will be shown to the larger social media community.

## UNDERSTANDING SOCIAL ALGORITHMS

There are many factors to consider within brand engagement. But it is absolutely important to understand the way social algorithms work and how they influence social media strategy. The *social algorithms* are mathematical equations designed to evaluate the quality of content posted by brands and determine which content receives more prominent placement in social media streams. Social media expert Rohit Bhargava (2012) illustrated the importance of social algorithms when he pointed out that 90% of Facebook users do not return to a fan page once they click the 'Like' button and only about 16% of a page's updates are seen by the page's fans. The goal of social media campaigns is to fully engage a brand community with relevant and thriving conversations with which they want to participate, and brands can only do this well if content is optimized and performing well according to social algorithms.

In order to understand social algorithms, we should first review the basic premise of search engine optimization (SEO), which gave the foundation for today's modern social media algorithms. Google, as one may expect, was the vanguard search engine to implement SEO algorithms (Page, 2015). The goal of Google was to sift through the millions of indexed web pages and provide a qualified result to people who were searching for information with Google.com. Strictly from a business standpoint, this was an incredibly strategic move for Google. Search engines have one commodity: to provide the best, most accurate results for what a user wants. If they are unable to do that, people will migrate to a different search engine. Google's algorithm revolutionized digital communications and caused industry professionals to begin a quest to understand SEO and its impact on organizational online communications. Bruce Clay, a leading SEO expert, defines SEO as: "the science/art of increasing traffic to a website by helping it rank higher in organic (non-paid) search results" (Bruce Clay Inc., n.d., "What is SEO?"). Applying this same concept to social media, *social media optimization involves the science and art of engaging online communities effectively to build strategic conversations within social media platforms among a brand community, causing organic (non-paid) content to show in the general streams of information for users.*

So what is included in the algorithm for social media? It is impossible to know all of the factors. For example, there are over 100,000 factors included in determining what shows in an individual's News Feed on

Facebook (McGee, 2013). Each user will have different stories show-ing in their News Feeds. Why so many factors? It is an indication of the maturing of the social media sites.

In 2009, Facebook first launched the News Feed feature for users but quickly found that the sheer amount of information was overwhelming. It contained every update, post, and status within the News Feed for each user. This led Ari Steinberg, a Facebook Engineer, to introduce the idea of News Feed Optimization (NFO) using an algorithm called Edge Rank. It had three main factors: $\Sigma = U_e W_e D_e$ (Patterson, 2015):

1. $U_e$ = Affinity, or the score of the connection between the user and the creator of the content.
2. $W_e$ = Weight, or the value for the type of action users take with the content. As previously mentioned, something like a comment would have more weight than a like.
3. $D_e$ = Decay, or the measurement of the time between when content is created and the individual may be seeing it.

Over the years, Facebook has made many changes to the algorithm in order to be more competitive with how users engage with content on the platform. Changes include adjustments such as: privileging links to qual-ity news sites in December 2013, increasing the exposure of text updates by friends of users in January 2014, expanding the reach for tagged con-tent among the connections of those who were tagged in February 2014, penalizing brands who posted content with little context in August 2014, highlighting trending content in the News Feed in September 2014, and penalizing overly promotional posts by organizations in November 2014 (Patterson, 2015). In addition, in 2015 Facebook further adjusted their NFO to help reduce hoaxes and to push content from friends of users higher in the News Feed (Lee, 2015). All of these are part of what Lars Backstrom, Engineering Manager for News Feed Ranking at Facebook, views as increasing the maturity of the algorithm:

> The easiest analogy is to search engines and how they rank web pages. It's like comparing the Google of today with Alta Vista. Both Google and Bing have a lot of new signals, like personalization, that they use. It's more sophisticated than the early days of search, when the words on a page were the most important thing.
>
> (as quoted in Page, 2015)

While every platform will have its own factors, there are similarities to keep in mind. For example, Pinterest relies on two main factors: Pin Quality and Source Quality. Note that the decay, or time-factor, is not as relevant on this platform (Page, 2015). In YouTube, a key factor to keep in mind is the total watch time of a video, not ultimately the views and clicks (Page, 2015). It is important, therefore, to understand what each social media platform values as part of the algorithm. While social media strategists cannot know each factor in an algorithm, as these are closely protected by social platforms and search engines, there are many indicators that give insight into what is important in social media content. Essentially, content that is relational and engaging tends to yield the highest impact in algorithms. In early 2016, both Twitter and Instagram started using algorithms as a way to optimize content for users. It is reasonable to presume that other platforms, such as Snapchat, may also follow suit.

It is very important to recognize the value of algorithms. If a social media campaign is being developed for an online community that has previously experienced a very poor interaction rate, thus having a low score in social algorithms, it will take some time to rebuild the brand's status in the social media platform's performance. That is highly relevant to note, as it will influence the kind of strategies and timing for content when creating a social media campaign.

Returning to the evaluation of the brand community's engagement, it is now possible to evaluate the interaction with a deeper expertise. Evaluate both the kind of engagement users have within a brand community and the genres of content that seem most valuable. One way to do this is by looking at the platform analytics.

### UNDERSTANDING PLATFORM ANALYTICS

While in-depth understanding of analytics for social media will be covered in the chapter on evaluation, it is helpful to highlight a few components that are particularly useful in the listening phase of a social media campaign. The goal in evaluating platform analytics at this stage is to understand which content has had the highest quality and quantity engagement. For example, in Facebook Insights, available to every official page on Facebook, it is possible to review key measurements. Identify whether there has been a day with particular growth in the number of likes, or, potentially, a decrease in the number of likes. Then, review the content posted that day to see what may have triggered those behaviors. It is also possible to review individual posts to see which ones led to the most likes, comments, or shares. In YouTube, review which videos have the highest estimated minutes watched or the subscriber content; this can identify which videos are building subscribers and which ones may be driving traffic away. In Twitter's analytics, evaluate which tweets have the highest impressions and engagement and what the interests of the brand's followers are in order to customize content even further.

Go through each one of the organization's existing platforms and analyze the information available. By the end of this analysis of community engagement, it is possible to identify what content is more valuable to users on each platform and what kinds of content are disengaging a brand community.

**Key Data Application:** Understanding a brand community audience and knowledge of the historical content distribution are only valuable when integrated with expertise in recognizing *how* the brand community responds to the communication. Engagement is crucial in order to evaluate the impact of social algorithms, implications for why content may or may not be appearing in prominent locations, and an overall assessment of the likelihood that certain kinds of content influence weightier or more valuable engagement by the brand community.

### Brand Dialogue

Another helpful component to review prior to developing a campaign is the brand's dialogue with the community. Beyond posting content, does the organization interact with users, respond to questions, or share content from the community? If so, how often and what is the time-gap between when a community member posts and the organization responds? As previously mentioned, many people expect an organization to respond within one hour (Gesenhues, 2013). While that may be unrealistic, particularly for organizations that do not have a dedicated staff member working on social media, it is helpful to determine if there are long gaps between engagements. This may be an indicator for why users are less likely to re-engage with social media content.

Today's social media communities do not simply desire to consume information from organizations. Rather, they want to actively participate in and produce information as well (Kaplan & Haenlein, 2010). Those who fall into this category of desiring to produce rather than just be a consumer are known as "Prosumers" (Toffler, 1980). Susan Gunelius (2010) describes the prosumer phenomenon like this: "Rather than simply 'consuming' products, people are becoming the voices of those products" (para. 4). She goes on to point out that "Prosumers are the online influencers that business leaders and marketers must not just identify but also acknowledge, respect and develop relationships with" to thrive in today's social world (para. 6). Clearly, if brands are not interacting with online communities that have a deep desire to engage and produce, treating them simply as consumers of whatever content the brand has posted, the opportunity to build relevant conversations within a brand community is drastically diminished.

**Key Data Application:** Responding to brand community engagement is just as important as the initial social media post. Brand dialogue analysis provides a platform to understand the ways in which the brand has historically interacted and allows for strategists to identify areas to increase, optimize, or develop within two-way conversations.

## Influencers

*Influencers* are the individuals on social media platforms that drive engagement, ignite dialogue around certain topics, and typically would be able to help expand a conversation. To identify influencers, see which users repeatedly show up in results for certain topics and keywords. Use the same listening tools discussed above for identifying keywords and topics in social platforms and then sort the data based on users. There are also several platforms designed with specific functions to easily identify influencers in social media. These platforms are generally based on an algorithm that calculates the engagement with individual user content and scores them on a level of "influence." A free platform that many people opt to use is Klout, though it has received criticism from the social media community due to the potential to influence a Klout score with spam-like tactics. Other options include Sprout Social, Brandwatch, Kred, Traackr, and UberVu. The primary objective of each of these platforms is to identify key influencers for topics of interest. Whether using a paid service or not, once an influencer is identified, there are a few more things to discover.

When developing an influencer list for each platform, create a file or database to easily tag the influencer with the keywords/phrases to which they relate. This will allow one to quickly identify which influencers may be interested in particular content that is being created. Additionally, know which platforms influencers are on, how many followers they have, and any other information or scoring metrics that are available, such as which other topics they like to discuss online, whether they are interacting with other brands already, and if the organization has followed/liked/connected with them (if not, be sure to do so). The goal is to have a full profile of these influencers in order to effectively build a relationship with them. Remember, people want to be prosumers . . . to create content. Influencers are those individuals who are already known for being thought leaders and conversation starters. A great component to keep in mind in laying the foundation for a social media campaign, therefore, is which influencers might be interested in participating with the brand's social initiatives.

**Key Data Application:** Within each brand community, there are key individuals who drive conversations forward and truly ignite connection. These influencers should be identified and specifically encouraged to participate within a campaign.

## Competition

One of the best things that can be done to strategize effective social media campaigns is to analyze competitors and other leaders within the industry. This gives insight into how organizations of similar vision and focus are performing within the social spaces.

Create a list of the key competitors and determine which social media sites they currently use. Go onto each platform and note the audience size and any other pertinent metrics. Consider using similar reviewing strategies for engagement as previously discussed for the brand's own page. There are several areas to note in this analysis. First, identify which platforms seem to be the most popular based on what is widely utilized within the organization's sector or industry. Second, note the type of audience engagement and size that is standard in the industry. There are a couple of tools to consider using in audience research. For example, in Facebook Insights, add competitors to the list "Pages to Watch" and keep track of the competition's likes and engagement. As with other social media functions, there are some tools that have options for competitive analysis including Rival IQ, Hootsuite Pro, Twitter Counter, and Simply Measured. The end goal of these efforts, whether an organization opts for a paid service or manual tracking, is to identify how the brand's engagement and community compare to that of the competition. Using this information, social media strategists are able to provide greater context for the decisions that will inform social media campaign design. Rather than solely looking at the brand's audience engagement and community reach in a vacuum, compare it to competitive standards among others in the social media landscape.

Another area to evaluate with competition is the design of their social media profiles. Consider what pieces of content they provide, the images they highlight and their use of rich media. It is useful to see what the strongest competitors are doing in the profile design as well as how under-performing competitors have set up their social presence. Be sure to compare these competitor findings to the current social media profiles of the brand in order to identify areas to enhance or change. In addition, review the kind of content the competitors are producing. Previously, the brand's own content was analyzed to calculate the percentage of originally produced content versus curated content, type of tone, media type, and other factors. Now review the same categories with the competition to see what kind of content seems to work the best for engagement and what patterns are observable in their content use.

Finally, analyze the brand's share of voice (SOV). Share of voice "essentially means comparing your crucial performance metrics against those of key competitors" (Weintraub, n.d., para. 1). In short, SOV is a metric that "details what percentage of mentions within your industry are about your brand, and what percentage is about the competition" (Torr, 2015, para. 2). For example, this can be accomplished by identifying key competitors and tracking how often they are mentioned in social media platforms compared to the brand's mentions. Or, track the organization's main keywords or phrases connected with reference to the brand, compared to those same keywords or phrases referencing competition.

To calculate share of voice, use an Excel spreadsheet or some other table feature. When representing SOV, calculate total mentions as well as create a pie chart to illustrate findings. First, tabulate all relevant references to the brand in the last 30 days. Include the tone of the comments, which can be highlighted by many social listening tools. Be sure to review the comments manually, as the tools identify the tone in comments based on an algorithm and not human intuition, which can lead to some confusion. For example, sarcasm may make a comment *appear* to have a positive tone when the person actually was upset with a brand (e.g. "So glad I waited an hour and still did not get a response from customer service. #FavoriteBrand"). Calculate all positive comments, negative comments, and neutral comments. In the final column, calculate share of voice mentions by adding the positive and neutral comments together. Finally, develop a pie chart that shows the percentages of share of voice broken down by each brand. This will give an idea of how often conversations

| Social Comments | Positive | Neutral | Share of Voice | Negative |
|---|---|---|---|---|
| Your brand | 50 | 15 | 65 | 5 |
| Competition 1 | 48 | 10 | 58 | 10 |
| Competition 2 | 30 | 5 | 35 | 0 |
| Competition 3 | 55 | 15 | 70 | 15 |

| Share of Voice Percent | |
|---|---|
| Your Brand | 28.51% |
| Competition 1 | 25.44% |
| Competition 2 | 15.35% |
| Competition 3 | 30.70% |
| *Total* | 100.00% |

**Share of Voice**

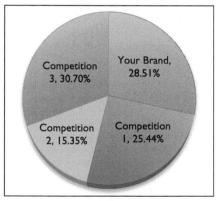

*Figure 2.4* Share of Voice Chart

that relate to the brand's industry or sector reference the organization and the brand's competition.

Next, perform the same activities for the top competitors. When all the numbers are gathered, create another chart that will show total *positive and neutral* mentions as SOV. Although the negative comments will not be useful in determining a positive share of the conversation being attributed to your brand, it may give insight into a change over time that reveals a better SOV for your brand. To calculate the percentage of SOV, divide the positive and neutral mentions each organization received by the total mentions for all brands that you assessed (Dunham, 2015).

Next, create an average sentiment chart. A *sentiment score* is a metric that communicates the strength or level of positive communication in social media from key publics regarding a brand. To calculate the sentiment value for each brand in the share of voice report, use the following equation from Jay Baer (n.d.):

(number of positive posts for the brand $\times$ 5) +
(number of neutral posts for the brand $\times$ 3) +
(number of negative posts for the brand $\times$ 1).

Take the number and divide it by the total number of mentions for all brands to arrive at a number between one and five. The closer the number is to five, the better a sentiment score is. From the average sentiment, it is possible to analyze what type of content competition may be using to yield a higher share of voice and also to provide a benchmark to compare against after a social media campaign (Dunham, 2015).

| Social Comments | Positive | Neutral | Negative | Total |
|---|---|---|---|---|
| Your Brand | 50 | 15 | 5 | 70 |
| Competition 1 | 48 | 10 | 10 | 68 |
| Competition 2 | 30 | 5 | 0 | 35 |
| Competition 3 | 55 | 15 | 15 | 85 |

| Sentiment Score = | (Positive Comments X 5)+ | (Neutral Comments X 3)+ | (Negative Comments X 1) | /Total Comments |
|---|---|---|---|---|

| Sentiment Scores | |
|---|---|
| Your Brand | 4.29 |
| Competition 1 | 4.12 |
| Competition 2 | 4.71 |
| Competition 3 | 3.94 |

*Figure 2.5* Sentiment Score Chart

Having gathered a large amount of data on the organization's background, mission, and communication processes, as well as a robust analysis of the social media landscape for the brand, the social media strategist must *apply* the information into purposeful and deliberate application for a campaign.

**Key Data Application:** Competition analysis allows brands to identify what type of content is generally the most effective across an industry, to identify engaging profile creation, and ultimately to evaluate the brand's share of voice and sentiment score within the social landscape. This information can then be used to inform specific tactical creation within a campaign as well as serving as a benchmark to evaluate the success of campaign messaging.

## Sense Making

Having a robust understanding of the organization, audience, platforms, and competition it is important to move into strategic use of that data. Sense-making is the crucial last component to the listening phase. Often, people are eager to jump into developing a campaign after gathering so much data. But unless the data is mined for information and that information is applied in meaningful ways to the context of a brand's social media needs, organizations will be unable to effectively leverage the power of social media for their brand.

### SWOT Analysis

A SWOT analysis is a common tool that assesses the strengths, weaknesses, opportunities, and threats for an organization. It will also develop a framework to understand how these four areas relate to each other. An example of how to set up the chart is provided below.

When considering what items to place in each box, there are several dimensions to keep in mind. First, think about the organizational strengths

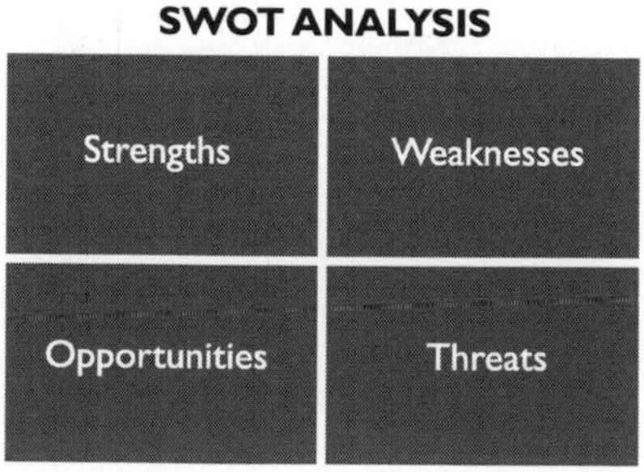

**SWOT ANALYSIS**

| Strengths | Weaknesses |
|-----------|------------|
| Opportunities | Threats |

*Figure 2.6* SWOT Matrix

and weaknesses and write them down in the first two boxes. These are the two *inward*-facing or organization-facing categories, relating to factors over which the brand has direct control or influence. For example, a strength could be that the management team is very supportive and invests resources into the social media efforts. On the other hand, a weakness might be that the organization has little online analysis available from the website or other initiatives in which to inform actions. Another example of a strength would be that the brand has highly loyal audiences who are already engaged online. Another weakness might be that, despite a highly loyal audience, the brand itself is relatively unknown, resulting in a rather small, though loyal, audience. Making a list of these factors will be the first step. Next, the opportunities and threats relate to external factors, or areas that are not in the direct control or influence of the brand. For example, there might be a significant opportunity in social media to provide real-time engagement to audiences. However, a threat could be that a competitor already has a strong social media presence and a majority of the share of voice.

Once the data is categorized into a SWOT diagram, make meaningful applications by using the quadrants. Each quadrant relates to the others to help analyze the data and apply it in meaningful ways to strategic design. For example, examining strengths in relation to opportunities provides the potential to develop strategies that take full advantage of the potential within social media. It is possible to also evaluate the weaknesses identified within the organization's social media to determine steps that can be taken to ensure that threats do not inhibit the social media campaign's potential. Below is a diagram of how to convert the raw data from a SWOT analysis into a meaningful application for a social media campaign.

|  | **Strengths** | **Weaknesses** |
|---|---|---|
| **Opportunities** | S-O Strategies: Approaches that utilize strengths to take advantage of opportunities. | W-O Strategies: Seek to overcome weaknesses in order to take full advantage of opportunities. |
| **Threats** | S-T Strategies: Discover ways to capitalize on strengths in order to minimize threats. | W-T Strategies: Identify and reduce weaknesses in order to prevent threats from inhibiting the organization. |

*Figure 2.7* SWOT Tactic Matrix

## Problem/Opportunity Statements

After identifying all the key pieces of background necessary, surveying the social landscape, and applying those findings into a SWOT analysis, it is now possible to create a problem or opportunity statement. This statement will help guide the social media campaign. In one to two sentences, capture the essence of what is going on with social media and why, at this time, the brand is creating a social media campaign. Write it in present tense (because it is happening now) and simply state what is going on—do not provide a solution or answer to the current problem/opportunity. This statement is an assessment of the current status in a brand's social media world.

Sometimes these statements fall into the genre of a "problem" statement. For example: "Current social media engagement with our online community is severely diminished, resulting in customer complaints." However, sometimes brand research identifies opportunities that are untapped in social media. For example, an opportunity statement might be: "Social media platforms currently provide 25% of the traffic to the website but result in 50% of the conversations for online traffic. There is opportunity to grow social media as a traffic source for our website beyond its current 25%." Whether writing a problem or opportunity statement, remember to keep it short. Make it present tense. Do not infer blame or indicate an "answer."

Now that a refined problem/opportunity statement has been developed, based out of in-depth research, it is possible to move into strategic design. This is the part of the campaign process where social media strategists propose data-informed solutions or responses to the current social media environment that the organization is experiencing.

### KEY CONCEPT SNAPSHOT

1.  Social media strategy directly relates to organizational vision and purpose. Be sure to do a complete review of the organization's key documents prior to developing a social media campaign.
2.  While strategy is a conduit to express the organization's vision, social media is a direct connection and relationship building process with key stakeholders. Understand the needs, values, interests, and conversations that are taking place among social media publics.
3.  Craft an opportunity or problem statement that specifies the intentionality of the organization's social media activities. This statement guides the campaign development.

## Suggested Reading

Bhargava, R. (2012). *Likeonomics: The unexpected truth behind earning trust, influencing behavior, and inspiring action.* Hoboken, NJ: John Wiley & Sons.

Coiné, T., & Babbitt, M. (2014). *A world gone social: How companies must adapt to survive.* New York: AMACOM, American Management Association.

Kerpen, D. (2011). *Likeable social media: How to delight your customers, create an irresistible brand, and be generally amazing on Facebook (& other social networks).* New York: McGraw-Hill.

## References

*Note:* All website URLs accessed on February 2, 2016.

Baer, J. (n.d.) How to create a share of voice report. *Convince and Convert.* Retrieved from: www.convinceandconvert.com/social-media-strategy/how-to-create-a-share-of-voice-report/

Bhargava, R. (2012). *Likeonomics: The unexpected truth behind earning trust, influencing behavior, and inspiring action.* Hoboken, NJ: John Wiley & Sons.

Brito, M. (2014). *Your brand, the next media company: How a social business strategy enables better content, smarter marketing, and deeper customer relationships.* Indianapolis, IN: Que.

Bruce Clay Inc. (n.d.). Search engine optimization – SEO tutorial. *BruceClay.com.* Retrieved from www.bruceclay.com/seo/search-engine-optimization.htm

Claussen, J. (2015, Feb. 9). Are you a social leader? Finding your blue unicorn. *ShoCase.com.* Retrieved from: http://corp.shocase.com/2015/02/social-leader-finding-blue-unicorn/

Coiné, T., & Babbitt, M. (2014). *A world gone social: How companies must adapt to survive.* New York: AMACOM, American Management Association.

Dunham, K. (2015, June). The beginner's guide to social media metrics: Share of voice. *UberVu.* Retrieved from: www.business2community.com/social-media/beginners-guide-social-media-metrics-share-voice-0856488#f5M35gmxDD457RLO.97

Gesenhues, A. (2013, Oct. 30). Study: 72% of consumers expect brands to respond within an hour to complaints posted on Twitter. *Marketing Land.* Retrieved from: http://marketingland.com/study-72-of-consumers-expect-brands-to-respond-within-an-hour-to-complaints-posted-on-twitter-63496

Gunelius, S. (2010, July 3). The shift from CONsumers to PROsumers. *Forbes.* Retrieved from: www.forbes.com/sites/work-in-progress/2010/07/03/the-shift-from-consumers-to-prosumers/

Kaplan, A. M., & Haenlein, M. (2010). Users of the world, unite! The challenges and opportunities of social media. *Business Horizons, 53*(1), 59–68.

Kerns, C. (2014). *Trendology: Building an advantage through data-driven real-time marketing.* New York, NY: Palgrave Macmillan.

Kerpen, D. (2011). *Likeable social media: How to delight your customers, create an irresistible brand, and be generally amazing on Facebook (& other social networks).* New York: McGraw-Hill.

Lee, K. (2015, July). Decoding the Facebook News Feed: An up-to-date list of the algorithm factors and changes. *BufferSocial*. Retrieved from: https://blog.bufferapp.com/facebook-news-feed-algorithm

McGee, M. (2013, Aug. 13). EdgeRank is dead: Facebook's news feed algorithm now has close to 100K weight factors. *Marketing Land*. Retrieved from: http://marketingland.com/edgerank-is-dead-facebooks-news-feed-algorithm-now-has-close-to-100k-weight-factors-55908

Page, M. (2015, March 11). Taking advantage of the Social Network algorithms. *Smart Insights*. Retrieved from: www.smartinsights.com/social-media-marketing/social-media-optimisation/social-network-algorithms/

Patterson, M. (2015, Jan. 26). Edgerank: A guide to the Facebook News Feed algorithm. *Sprout Social*. Retrieved from: http://sproutsocial.com/insights/facebook-news-feed-algorithm-guide/

Toffler, A. (1980). *The third wave: The classic study of tomorrow*. New York: Bantam Books.

Torr, D. (2015). 4 ways to increase your share of voice on social media. *Hootsuite*. Retrieved from: http://blog.hootsuite.com/how-to-increase-share-of-voice/

Weintraub, M. (n.d.). The definitive share of voice guide: PPC, SEO, social & multi-channel SOV models. *aimClear*. Retrieved from: www.aimclearblog.com/2013/09/06/the-definitive-share-of-voice-guide-ppc-seo-social-multi-channel-sov-models/

# Chapter 3

# Step 2A: Strategic Design

## Developing a Data-Informed Social Media Campaign

> Respect for the nature and potential of social media demands that organizations approach engagement with intentionality and data-informed designs to develop trusted and authentic relationships.

After gathering the formative research from the listening phase and going through the sense-making process to develop a data-informed problem/opportunity statement, the next stage involves mapping out the overall strategy for the organization's social media. Before designing individual, shorter-term campaigns, first an organization must solidify the overall purpose and approach to social media. If this is not already in place, a social media professional should first start by developing a *social media strategic plan* that is the guiding framework for all campaigns and initiatives by the brand in social media.

## Social Media Strategic Plan

### Social Media Goals

With the full weight of the background about the company's vision, the current social media presence of the organization, and the potential audience, it is possible to effectively establish the goals for a brand's social media presence. Goals can be defined as "broad, summative statements that spell out the overall outcomes of the program" (Broom & Sha, 2013, p. 270). They essentially state where the brand plans to end up as a result of social media efforts. An example of a social media goal may be: "Become a thought-leader in social media for the technology industry." Another example could be: "Be recognized as a premier source for information and resources on non-profit philanthropy." When crafting the goal for social media, keep in mind the organization's overall mission or vision statement. A social media goal should directly relate to the purpose or mission of the brand, extending or enhancing the likelihood that the organization's overall vision will be accomplished. Once the goal is established, move into specific social media platform plans.

### Social Media Vision Statements

Once the goal of a brand's social media is identified, it is important to create *vision statements* for each platform that zero in on the value and purpose of each social media channel for the organization. To do this, identify each social media platform that is beneficial for the organization. This identification comes from research gathered during the listening phase where social media channels were reviewed based on keyword activity. It may have been that certain platforms were identified that did not have conversations relevant for the organization, resulting in very few conversations taking place that related to keywords. Or perhaps there are other platforms that were highly relevant but not yet in use by the brand. Create a list of all platforms that will be incorporated as a regular part of the brand's social media presence. In determining which platforms are important, consider the capabilities of the platform, the general audience it serves, the research regarding conversations on the platform, and details from the competitive analysis.

With identified social media channels in hand, it is important to create social media platform vision statements. In order to fully craft a vision statement, be sure to identify the capabilities of each platform. For example, Facebook has a strong advertising option, video integration, photo albums, etc. Instagram, on the other hand, has shorter video options and is mainly driven by individual visuals. Snapchat has the potential for stories as well as individual snaps. When you identify the potential *uses* of each platform, it is possible to specify how these specific platforms play into the overall goal of the organization and to craft a platform vision statement to guide future strategy.

The vision statements should include "the description of each social media profile's purpose, and how this purpose contributes to your business goals" (Sorokina, 2014). The value of identifying these areas is to strategically develop social media content and campaigns while unifying the approach to various platforms. Olsy Sorokina, a social media expert, suggests using the model of: "We will use *(social network)* for *(purpose of this social network)* in order to help *(business goal)*" (2014, para. 6). Examples of this could include: "We will use Facebook for advertising to target a specific audience in order to help increase sales" (Sorokina, 2014, para. 8), or "We will use Instagram for promoting and sharing our company culture to help with recruitment and employee happiness" (para. 14). In this way, a vision statement should be developed for each of the brand's social media sites.

### Creating SMART Objectives

With an end-purpose in view and vision statements for each platform, social media strategists are now ready to create objectives for the social media strategic plan. An objective can be defined as "specific knowledge,

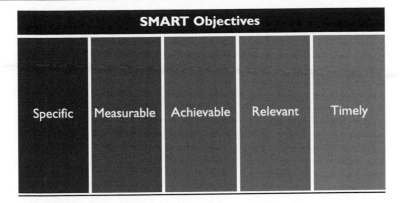

| SMART Objectives | | | | |
| --- | --- | --- | --- | --- |
| Specific | Measurable | Achievable | Relevant | Timely |

*Figure 3.1* SMART Objectives

opinion, and behavior outcomes to be achieved for each well-defined target publics, what some call 'key results'" (Broom & Sha, 2013, p. 270). Essentially, an *objective* is what will be measured as a key progress indicator (KPI) showing that a campaign goal is being met. Within the context of social media, identify the precise platform and the behavior or activities of the audiences that the brand would like to see as a result of these social media efforts.

It is important to draft these objectives in a way that provides parameters and accountability for social media engagement by using the acronym: SMART. This stands for specific, measurable, achievable, relevant, and timely. Each objective that is created should have all of these elements present. For example, a SMART social media objective might be: "Have 30 retweets a week as a result of posting to Twitter twice a day." The "specific" element to this objective is that it applies solely to Twitter. The "measurable" element is that there should be 30 retweets. Knowing how large the current Twitter audience is and the engagement history would clarify whether the measurable element is truly "achievable" as part of the objective. This may be an objective the brand will have to build toward to achieve, or it may be incredibly realistic based on research. "Relevant" will relate to the vision statement for Twitter and by evaluating what should be accomplished by those retweets. For example, it is relevant if the vision statement for Twitter by the brand included content that was designed to be shared or develop engagement. It could be that 30 retweets leads to reaching the awareness of a larger audience, or potentially enhancing the likelihood that people are clicking the link in that tweet and going to a website. Whatever the brand's purpose is for Twitter, make sure that the specific objective relates in a tangible way to achieving the vision. Finally, the example is "timely" as it has a one-week parameter for the retweets. Each week, it would reset and the brand could evaluate whether this objective was reached.

*Outcome-Based Objectives*

It is important to note that objectives should also be *outcome-based*. This means an objective is about what happens on the platform and within the brand community as a result of social media engagement. For example, in the illustration above, posting twice a week is an *output*. It is something that the organization will do. However, the 30 retweets will be an *outcome*. Those retweets are the result of the social media activities by brand community members. Ensuring that each objective is an outcome allows for higher accountability in social media program evaluation, which will be discussed in the evaluation section later. It is worth noting, however, that evaluation of objectives is used to illustrate the effectiveness and value of a social media campaign. The ability to evaluate a campaign rests heavily on developing SMART, *outcome-based objectives*. There is no authentic measurement of brand communities' engagement in social media when outputs are used as the measurement—it simply indicates that the social media team had a lot of activity. What should be measured is the impact, or results, of the efforts within social media platforms. In order to do that effectively, each objective must be SMART and outcome-based.

### Social Profile Branding

The next steps to take in a social media strategic plan are to ensure that all the organization's profiles are fully filled out, properly branded, and maintain a strong presence among online communities. The purpose of this is not just to fill in the information and make it look nice. The focus should be on a unifying brand presence as well as optimizing social media accounts. Here are some basic elements to consider:

*About Section*

The About section in each social profile is an opportunity to introduce the brand. Keep in mind the keywords and phrases developed in the social media listening stage, the marketing department's branding guideline, and the platform's audience. When writing the About sections, have a consistent presentation so that audiences feel like the brand is the same organization no matter which platform they are currently using. In addition, be strategic with wording in order to capitalize on search engine optimization opportunities. With search engines pulling more content in from social media sites, particularly with the partnership between Google and Twitter that began in 2015, using each phrase and posting strategically is vital for brands. Neil Patel (2015), co-founder of Crazy Egg, Hello Bar, and KISSmetrics, explains: "Social and search have intertwined into a squirming nexus of who's-where-and-who's-who" ("Social Search," para. 1). The About section provides a platform to share who the brand is and what they are all about with the online brand communities.

*Profile Photos and Thumbnails*

It seems like social media profile image sizes are constantly changing. Be sure to regularly review the social channels of a brand to ensure that images are crisp, properly sized, engaging, and branded. While each platform does not need the exact same photos, it is helpful to consider the general branding guidelines and applications of images across platforms. Some platforms, like Facebook, can gain more engagement when regularly changing a cover image. It might be something to consider updating with various initiatives or campaigns. But even when rotating those images, be sure to keep the feel of the brand in mind. Users should still recognize each cover photo as being from the brand or organization. Thumbnail images should be easily recognizable as well. Consider using the logo, as that is often the image associated with posts or comments. Have it created and sized specifically for each social media outlet. An easy way to identify the latest size requirements is to quickly search the Internet for an updated listing of each platform's image dimensions.

*Vanity URLs*

Customizing an organization's URL for each platform makes it easy for people to connect. A *vanity URL* is a unique, individualized URL for social platforms. For example, facebook.com/CarolynMaeKim is far easier to remember and share than facebook.com/149272585126883. When creating vanity URLs for an organization's social platforms, keep them consistent. Ideally, have one URL for all social media properties. Twitter tends to have less space, so it is a good idea to make a vanity URL for Twitter first and then apply that to other platforms. A helpful website to quickly check if a vanity URL is available across the social media landscape is www.Namechk.com.

*Company Connections*

One of the weakest points for many organizations is the connection between social platforms as well as the connection with the organization's website. Be sure to have the correct URL provided for the organization's main site, as well as incorporating the connections to other social profiles within each social media channel. It is helpful at this stage to also review the organization's website and ensure that the social media channels are easily identified on the homepage and other key locations. If they are not, connect with the website development team to ensure all channels are properly added on the website. This permits users to easily connect in multiple places, as well as allowing the community to quickly identify where they will be able to engage with the brand. For example, people should be able to get to the brand's Twitter profile from the website's homepage or they should easily be able to share a blog from the website to their Facebook News Feed. On Facebook, users should be able to connect over to the Instagram profile or YouTube channel. It should be a well-organized and clearly defined web of connections.

## Rich Media

When developing social profiles, also consider the inclusion of rich media. For example, on Twitter there are six locations for images or video that show on the main profile. It is advisable to add at least these six pieces of rich media to the Twitter profile before it goes live so the brand's profile presence appears complete. Instagram has a regular rotation of images across the profile background. It is helpful to make sure the brand has enough images that, as they rotate in and out, it appears diverse and interesting, rather than under-developed. Review each platform to understand how it displays, what media is needed, and where it is used. After this, develop branded pieces that can meet those needs to fully utilize each platform. If the brand is unsure what kind of media-rich content pieces to create, it can be helpful to reflect on the brand community conversations and keywords for the organization. Find images, video, infographics, and other rich media that involve these topics of mutual interest. That is what the brand community cares about and with which they will engage. Remember, the social principle is about identifying topics of mutual interest with a brand's audience and engaging in a conversation.

## Content Distribution

After each profile has a mission statement and is fully up-to-speed with the profile design, consider the content distribution strategy for the organization. The first step in a distribution plan is to create a content topic guide. Hootsuite's Senior Director of Social Media, Jaime Stein, provides a model for organizations on social media, which essentially allocates various percentages of social media content to specific focuses of the organization (LePage, 2014, "Create a Content Plan," para. 4). This is illustrated by the following example provided by Evan LePage of Hootsuite ("Create a Content Plan," para. 4): "50% of your content will drive back to the blog; 25% of your content will be curated from other source; 20% of your content will drive enterprise content; 5% of your content will be HR and culture." The percentages identified in the example are just that: an example. Each organization needs to create the content distribution guide percentages based on the brand's objectives and social media purpose. However, some organizations may not be in a place to know how to develop such defined metrics yet. It could be that more time is needed in social media before that can be solidified. If that is the case, brands may opt for the Rule of Thirds. The Rule of Thirds is essentially that one third of the content will be about the brand, one third will be shared from industry thought leaders, and one third will be dedicated to individual interactions with a brand community on social media.

Beyond the base allocation of percentage for content information, it is also helpful to create a general content calendar. A general content calendar guides the overall social media communication pieces and allows for harmonization across platforms. Much more specific content calendars are developed for each campaign. However, the general content calendar provides a framework to develop specific campaigns and also align communication with the overall brand's other communiqué pieces to audiences. A general content calendar should include:

- Platforms
- Day and, if possible, time of posts
- Keywords or topic of the post
- Category of content topic design
- Any media needed (images, photos, etc.)
- Team member responsible for post.

If the organization already uses a master content calendar for communication across all platforms (such as newsletters, website blogs, press releases), it is helpful to coordinate in order to ensure that social media complements the overall organizational communication patterns. Knowing what the organization is communicating in general will help social media strategists tailor content that is appropriate for each social channel.

### Social Media Voice

With a general content distribution guide in place and calendar created, develop the social media voice for the brand. This will include key messages and a message map that will guide how the organization interacts on social media and ensure that the brand persona is highlighted in all types of engagement. Before determining *what* to say and how to say it, having a strong brand persona is crucial. *Social media voice* is composed of understanding the brand's persona, the appropriate tone for a message, and the intentional language needed to effectively communicate in each post.

### Understanding Brand Persona

Style guides and brand voice are often captured in marketing style guidelines. The reality, however, is that many organizations have trouble translating those marketing guidelines into social media or, perhaps, they simply choose not to consider those guidelines. This becomes quite problematic. A brand's presentation on social media influences key publics' perceptions of the brand itself. It is not just a "social media" activity—it

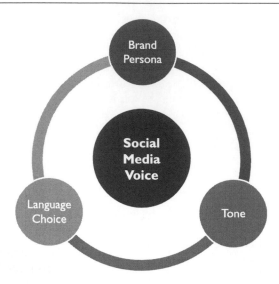

*Figure 3.2* Developing a Social Media Voice

directly impacts the organization's reputation and perception. It is, there-fore, crucial that the brand persona and style is maintained so that all social media efforts support the overall vision of the organization. Brian Solis (2010), social media guru, points out:

> In social networks, the brand and how it's perceived, is open to pub-lic interpretation and potential misconception now more than ever. Without a deliberate separation between the brand voice and person-ality and that of the person representing it, we are instantly at odds with our goals, purpose, and potential stature.
>
> (para. 7)

Strategic social media messaging involves more than just coming up with the right words. It is about understanding what the brand symbolizes and the persona of the brand into the digital sphere (Solis, 2010). When identifying a brand's persona, consider what kind of person the brand would be if it came to life. The organization may have a thoughtful brand persona or, perhaps, the brand persona would be more appropriate to the organization if it was somewhat playful or adventurous. Perhaps the organization's brand is lighthearted or perhaps it is academic. Determine what the brand's persona is before developing key messaging. Keep in mind, no matter what the persona, it still needs to be a humanized con-cept. Paul Armstrong (2011), emerging technology expert, says "Brands need to be human (in some form or another) if they want to succeed online" (para. 2).

## Tone

After identifying the brand's persona, establish the kind of tone that should come across in communication. Tone can be defined as "the underlying vibe that emanates from your brand's communications" (Schwab, 2015, "Tone"). The tone should reflect the brand persona and be uniquely appropriate to the specific audience the brand is engaging. Some brands might have a more personable tone, where others might take on a more direct or academic tone. When developing the key traits of a brand's social voice tone, consider not only the current type of communication tone by the brand, but also where the brand would like to see the social media conversations develop. Perhaps the tone will be more quiet and humble if the brand is in a new platform, but, after gaining credibility, will develop into more of an authoritative or scientific tone in the future. Understanding where the brand is today, where the brand hopes to be tomorrow, as well as the long-term objectives of the brand in social media, will determine the proper tone in the right context (Armstrong, 2011).

## Intentional Language

Keeping in mind the brand persona and tone, consider the purpose, or reason, for the communication. This should relate back to the social media campaign objectives. Recognize the purpose of the social media content, and think of the specific language that should be used. This concept will be developed further within the key messages and message map creation. Stephanie Schwab (2015), CEO and founder of Crackerjack Marketing, describes the challenge of developing language to match a social media voice by writing:

> Although your brand may be the expert in its field, coming off sounding like you're smarter than your customers could turn people off pretty quickly. Establishing appropriate brand language will give you a foundation for the types of words, phrases and jargon to be used in social media communications. Want to sound very exclusive? Use insider language and acronyms. Want to sound hip? Stay up-to-date on the latest slang. But be careful – if you make a misstep in slang it'll look like you're trying too hard.
>
> ("Language")

Learning to craft appropriate content is part of designing a strong social media voice. The key to effectively crafting appropriate content is remembering to base the design on the brand's persona and tone, as well as applying insight from the formative research on what causes audiences to engage and what the purpose of social media for the brand is.

Finally, before moving on to create social media campaigns, ensure that certain policies and procedures are in place. The four that will be discussed in this section are: 1) A social media community policy, 2) an employee social media use policy, 3) a policy for the social media teams within an organization, and 4) a crisis plan for social media.

### Social Media Community Policy

The goal of having a social media user policy is to protect the online community and the quality of conversations that take place in social media. A *community policy* is a document that outlines the kinds of behaviors that are welcome in the brand community, as well as negative behaviors and the consequences of those. Obviously, the nature of social media is such that a brand cannot control all conversations, nor should they try. However, it is important to have a policy in place that addresses certain kinds of interaction or communication that may be harmful to social media engagement and communities. A good place to start would be to reference whether the organization's website has a user policy in place for comments on blogs and other locations online.

Craft a social media community policy with the values of the organization and online brand community in mind. There are three main parts to include: 1) the values of the online community and the type of behavior that creates an environment where those values are seen, 2) behaviors that may inhibit the values of the community, and 3) actions that will be taken about comments/posts/etc. that violate those values.

### Values of the Community

As with anything in social media, the goal of the brand should be to inspire and engage—not dictate. With that in view, it is important that the beginning of a social media community policy focuses on what the purpose of the community is and how that can be accomplished. For example, remind people that every day thousands of users are having conversations that engage, connect, and inform mutual interests. Next, clarify the vision for the brand's platform and how that vision will enhance and expand the conversations that are meaningful to the community. For example, the brand may identify that the purpose of the Twitter account is to provide answers and resources for the brand community. Perhaps the value of the Facebook page is to provide a community for brand advocates to connect, share stories, and provide feedback for the brand. Whatever the goal is, it should be identified for users. Then, connect how that goal can be achieved with specific platform behaviors. For example, the brand might identify that, because the specific social site is a place to share stories, users are welcome to share their experiences and feedback. It would also be good to note that the brand might be unable to respond to each and every post due to the volume but that the brand values the conversations and wants the platform to be a place where that type of feedback takes place. There are a number of strong examples of social media user policies available online for easy reference.

### Types of Behavior that May Inhibit the Values

The next area to address in a user policy is the kinds of actions that may inhibit the values and purpose of the online community. In other words, are there certain kinds of engagement that the brand would delete if they are present in places like comments on Facebook posts or on a YouTube channel? Comments may include things like racial slurs, explicit or inappropriate language, or personal threats against other users. Identify the *exact* kinds of behaviors that are not appropriate and why those behaviors directly conflict with the platform's values and purpose. Ultimately, the focus of a community policy, also sometimes called a social media user policy, is to foster a strong environment within the social media platform. If community members are threatening that goal, they need to understand how their behavior is harmful and why it does not support the values of the community. A great example can be seen in the Mayo Clinic's Participation Guidelines (n.d.). After setting up some basics about the platforms and encouraging participation in the online conversations, the Mayo Clinic says: "We also expect a basic level of civility; disagreements are fine, but mutual respect is a must, and profanity or abusive language are out-of-bounds" (para. 2). The idea is that, while conversation is encouraged, there are certain behaviors that would actually limit the overall communication climate of the online community.

### Consequences of Behavior

Finally, specify how the organization will respond when behaviors do not foster the values of the community. Be very clear in this section. The reason is it allows everyone to be on the same page if the brand does, in fact, end up needing to delete comments, block users, or report content. Having a policy in place early on means that, if the brand has to respond to content in one of these ways, the organization cannot be accused of censoring or being biased against certain views. Rather, it will be clear to everyone in the social media community that, from the very beginning, the organization had set values; identified behaviors that support those values, and specific behaviors that are not appropriate in the social media platforms; and set responses to inappropriate behaviors.

## EXPERT INSIGHT

*Matt Prince*

**What do you think is one hallmark competency social media professionals need to succeed?**

Being a storyteller. This is one of the most powerful aspects to any brand and/or individual. Fundamental human behavior has not changed when it comes to marketing, but the way we do it has. Keeping that in mind is key to the underlying importance of connecting on an emotional level and doing it in an authentic way.

**What role does brand persona and tone play in developing a social media campaign for a brand?**

Good social media campaigns have a developed voice, while great social media campaigns incorporate tone. Voice defines your brand personality, while tone reflects your specific audience.

**What are some ways brands can stay engaging and interesting on social media with so many organizations already launching incredible campaigns?**

The most important way for brands to maintain interest is to stay relevant and true to their audience. Authenticity is the strongest currency a brand can have. Communications should be grounded in truth and differentiated by the emotional connection. It's important to remember choices by consumers are not made by function alone, but are driven by emotion.

**What role should social media advertising play within a campaign?**

Social platforms are making it harder and harder for brands to organically reach their audiences. Whether it's through sponsored posts or paid influencers, social media has established itself as a valuable business driver, and its increasing budgets are reflecting that.

**Is it possible for organizations to develop employee social media policies that empower? If so, what are those key ingredients?**

Companies no longer have a social media team of one or two—it's as big as their entire workforce. Each employee has the ability to share, leak, promote, defend, and deter your brand. Empowered employees can be a remarkable social tool for brands, but that isn't built in the social media policy. It's developed in the company culture and shared through social media.

**What are the core elements of a strong social media campaign goal?**

Measurability is key to any campaign and social media is no exception. Whether it's sales overnight or brand overtime, all social campaigns should have clear objectives that are measurable.

**What are the key ethical areas that brands should keep in mind on social media?**

Policies and laws are quickly catching up to the dynamic economy of social media. Making sure brands are up to date on influencer promotions, legal repercussions, accuracy, credibility, and privacy is key to ensuring ethical social media success.

**Connect with Matt:** @Matt_Prince | https://www.linkedin.com/in/mattprince1 | https://www.facebook.com/matthewprince

*Matt Prince is the PR + Newsroom Manager at Taco Bell*

### Employee Social Media Policies

Social media policies for employees are a growing area of focus for organizations. Employees can be a brand's biggest advocates and fans in the social world, and they should be empowered. However, organizations also need to provide some guidance for appropriate social media usage, particularly with the growing saturation of social media use in personal and professional contexts. It is recommended that the employee social media policies are added to the employee handbook, incorporated into new employee training, and added into regular employee training meetings to remind the organization about the ways that social media impacts the workplace. A social media policy for employees should empower, build trust, and guide. This kind of policy, however, tends to be the most difficult to write. Beyond working to be sure that the organization is empowering and not stifling, it is also vital to work very closely with the legal team to make sure that the brand is not violating any employee rights.

### National Labor Relations Act and Social Media

The National Labor Relations Act has several areas that apply directly to the types of policies an organization can have for social media use. For example, section seven says:

> Employees have the right to unionize, to join together to advance their interests as employees, and to refrain from such activity. It is unlawful for an employer to interfere with, restrain, or coerce employees in the exercise of their rights.
>
> (National Labor Relations Board, n.d.a, "Interfering with Employee Rights," para. 1)

Essentially, this means that communication by employees that deals with matters such as working conditions, their pay, and interest to advance themselves as employees in a joint effort, are protected. Businesses and organizations cannot create social media policies that would discipline that kind of communication. In fact, some organizations that fired employees over social media communication that falls into this genre of content have been required to reinstate them. The National Labor Relations Board (NLRB) has also required organizations to adjust their policies due to the requirements being overly broad. These kinds of cases are nothing new—in fact, the NLRB began reviewing and providing memos of cases dealing with employees and social media policies in 2011. They identified two main areas to keep in mind: "Employer policies should not be so sweeping that they prohibit the kinds of activity protected by federal labor law, such as the discussion of wages or working conditions among employees" and "an employee's comments on social media are generally not protected if they are mere gripes not made in relation to group activity among employees" (National Labor Relations Board, n.d.b, "The NLRB and Social Media," para. 6).

Keeping in mind the protection of employees to make concerted efforts in a group toward better working conditions, there are parameters that can be placed. For example, there are legal policies organizations have regarding harassing other employees, releasing proprietary information, and other kinds of behaviors that intersect with existing HR and legal requirements. On April 16, 2015 the NLRB concluded that a social media policy by Landry's Inc. was legal and upheld employees' rights while also providing guidelines of how social media behaviors may influence existing legal policies by the organization. Their policy provides an excellent example to consider for employee policy design. Part of the policy stated:

> While your free time is generally not subject to any restriction by the Company, the Company urges all employees not to post information regarding the Company, their jobs, or other employees which could lead to morale issues in the workplace or detrimentally affect the Company's business. This can be accomplished by always thinking before you post, being civil to others and their opinions, and not posting personal information about others unless you have received their permission. You are personally responsible for the content you

publish on blogs, wikis, or any other form of social media. Be mindful that what you publish will be public for a long time. Be also mindful that if the Company receives a complaint from an employee about information you have posted about that employee, the Company may need to investigate that complaint to insure that there has been no violation of the harassment policy or other Company policy. In the event there is such a complaint, you will be expected to cooperate in any investigation of that complaint, including providing access to the posts at issue.

(National Labor Relations Board, 2015, p. 3)

As has been illustrated, it is highly advisable to work closely with HR and the legal team to compose an employee social media policy. As the policy is shaped, keep in mind the goals: empower, build trust, and guide.

### Empower

The first thing to do in a social media policy for employees is to empower them. Ideally, they will love where they work and want to talk about the great things with which they are involved. Coca-Cola, for example, created their social media principles to help employees be empowered. After noting that there are more than 150,000 associates in 200 companies that may be engaging in the social media world, Coca-Cola writes, "Have fun, but be smart. Use sound judgment and common sense, adhere to the Company's values, and follow the same Company policies that you follow in the offline world" (Coca-Cola, n.d., "Social Media Principles," para. 3). Leading by example, Coca-Cola then identifies the values that will guide the brand's social media interaction including: transparency of communication, protection of privacy, respecting the rights of others, responsible use of technology, and monitoring their behavior for appropriate records of interaction. Coca-Cola also has five key points for their employees on social media including reminding them about policies that influence employee behavior, disclosing their work status if they are promoting information regarding the company on social media, and being conscientious about their personal social media use while at work ("Personal Use of Social Media").

Another great example of an employee social media policy comes from Kodak's "Social Media Tips" document (2010). Kodak provided these tips to empower strong use of social media by organizations. They identify ten rules that help guide their employee social media in two general areas: reputation, and privacy (pp. 10–11). In addition to the guides for their employees, they also created details on each platform and some basic Q and A sections to assist users who may be less familiar with each platform. This is a great way to empower employees not only to understand *how* to share but also to know the functionality of the platforms themselves.

*Build Trust*

Social media policies for employees are not about a brand's attempt to control those who work for them, but rather about creating online communities that are positive experiences for everyone. It is important, therefore, that your employees recognize the intention behind a social media policy. To build trust it is helpful to include the values of the organization itself on social media, perhaps even referencing the overall goal of why the organization is in social media in the first place. It can also help to remind people about what will *not* be required—for example, the organization should not require that employees become their manager's "friends" on Facebook, or that all employees have to follow the brand on Instagram or Twitter.

In addition, create specific things to help encourage employees on social media—perhaps highlight the top "brand advocates" in an employee meeting or recognize outstanding contributions to community conversations in the social world. Employees are an incredibly valuable part of any organization—both in the online world and offline world. Building trust requires that the organization not only empower employees to be brand ambassadors on behalf of the organization, but also that the organization recognizes the employees' value and contribution to the online community in the same way that any other brand influencer would be recognized. It all goes back to being relational and human, not coercive and dictatorial.

*Guide*

The Guide part of the social media plan is helpful to allow employees to understand how their workplace policies may affect online interaction. For example, while there is a certain level of free speech and concerted employee activity allowed, disclosure of confidential information may also be harmful. If an organization is an educational institution, there are legal requirements set out by the Federal Education Rights and Privacy Act that prohibit disclosure of student information. This act applies online in the same way it would in person. To help, an organization may want to give examples in the employee guidelines that illustrate appropriate ways to celebrate and recognize students they work with, and inappropriate ways that may violate FERPA. There may also be organizations that have products in development that require employees and contractors to sign non-disclosure documents. Again, employees need to understand not just how that non-disclosure agreement applies to in-person conversation settings, but online as well. For example, employees may not realize that their location may be disclosed when uploading to certain social media sites. It is helpful to remind them of that function if the organization has any work in undisclosed locations. These types of examples depend highly on the kind of organization. That is why it is helpful to be sure to customize an employee social media policy specifically for the organization itself.

## Social Media Brand User Policy

The final type of user policy that needs to be in place is the social media policy for the individuals who will be running the actual brand's social media account. There are countless examples of brands that have had disasters from their own social media accounts. The goal of an internal social media brand user policy is to prevent these kinds of situations.

When creating a brand user policy, it is extremely important to have buy-in from all parties that will be involved. It is advisable to work with the groups together in creating the policy so that all needs are met and everyone involved supports the process. Within any organization, there will be many parties interested in getting information out via social media. There may be a marketing team, a sales team, a PR team, a community relations team, and management. The social media strategists will also likely need to consult with leadership, HR, and, at times, legal, on what is posted. The brand user policy should account for the needs and requirements from all these groups.

### Roles

An internal brand user policy should clearly identify roles. For example, who will be the main contact for social media questions that need to go to legal? When multiple groups need to get information into social media channels, who is the lead on collecting those requests and getting back to the various groups? Will HR be involved with all posts that involve anything around an employee, or only specific ones? Working together with all parties on addressing these questions will allow everyone to feel comfortable and committed to the social media process. It also will incorporate the expertise of each of these areas, which will enhance the effectiveness of the policy.

In addition to points of contact, a social media team also needs to identify the roles of content creation and delivery. Be clear about who is responsible for posting the content and on which channels; who will be responsible for monitoring and reporting on the content interaction; and who the lead social media person will be. The director or manager may be tasked with the strategy behind campaigns and content, allowing them to be the decision maker when multiple requests come in simultaneously. It will be their responsibility to harmonize the needs of groups into one communication message through social media and to manage the other team members who are implementing the actual components of a campaign into the social media world.

### Branding and Platforms

While already identified, a consolidated explanation of branding requirements and logo use is helpful to include in the social media brand user policy. It allows anyone who is involved with the brand's social media to understand what is and is not the appropriate application of colors, fonts, slogans, and trademarks. It is also important to incorporate the social media voice within this portion so that people understand the tone and approach to use when interacting on social media. Within this document, list the platforms that the brand is on, the usernames, and the vanity URLs associated with those accounts. The document should not, however, include passwords as the social media director will want to maintain access only for those individuals directly responsible for posting on that platform. It is also advisable to include the content distribution strategy so that all users understand the genres of content and ultimate goals for the platforms. While these sections will be abbreviated from the larger social media strategic plan, discussed above, it is helpful to reference each area for familiarity. Also provide access to the entire social media strategic plan to gain a more robust understanding of the organization's approach to social media as well as the policies that guide activities in working for the brand's social media team.

### White Papers

A final part that is highly recommended for a brand's social media user policy is "white papers." These are often not included in the official social media brand user policy but can be kept in the same area. White papers can be created on each platform the brand is currently using, addressing current platform basics such as audience size and known functionality; proprietary information such as traditional performance and the audience profile; and any platform-specific guidelines, such as partners on the platform used for cross-promotion, advertising policies, etc. White papers can easily be updated as platforms change and develop. This is helpful as updating the official social media brand user policy is much more involved and requires representatives from various departments. White papers, on the other hand, should be more fluid as they require constant updating to reflect platform specifications and requirements. The white papers do not incorporate approval processes, responsibilities, and other areas that require joint agreement. Rather, they simply provide guidance based on specific social media properties.

### Crisis Plan

While the approach to dealing with a social media crisis will be addressed later, it is important to note that every social media team needs to have a crisis plan on file. This crisis plan should have a direct connection with the organization's overall crisis plan. Usually, the public relations department will already have a crisis plan created. Meeting with them to discuss specific applications, roles, and approval processes for social media posting during a crisis is important. Key areas to identify include: 1) how social media will be used during a crisis that was created outside of social media; and 2) what roles the public relations team will play or what approval processes they will implement during crises created as a result of something happening on social media. Often crises arise externally of social media and are caused as a result of something internal with the brand. Perhaps there were mass lay-offs, maybe a product caused harm to someone, or potentially a natural disaster impacted the brand. But at other times social media is the direct cause of the crisis itself, such as an employee posting an inappropriate picture or a customer's tweet about a negative experience going viral. A crisis plan will need to address both types of situations.

One thing to keep in mind when drafting the plan is having a process in place for approval of content during a crisis. Often, in a crisis, legal and HR may be involved. However, the nature of social media is that it moves extremely quickly and so a brand cannot afford to simply be quiet for hours on end within a social context while teams go through numerous approval processes. As a team, in addition to understanding approval process and time-lines for specific crisis information that could be released through an event, also develop a plan for the kinds of social responses that can be posted quickly without causing legal problems. It is helpful to consider creating pre-approved crisis posts that can be both customized for the specific situation and then used to direct people to a set platform for updates, such as a company blog, which would be maintained by the PR team during a crisis. In addition, most organizations have a crisis team that will be called during any major event. Consider asking whether the social media director may be part of the team, or if the social media strategist can have direct access to a key decision maker on the crisis response team who will be able to give approval for social media content.

If a crisis is caused as a result of social media, it is also helpful to have a key group of people in place that can be called on for advice and direction. These contacts, and their roles and titles, should be identified in the crisis plan. When a crisis erupts as a result of social media, brands need to quickly respond. If it was a rogue post accidentally sent from the company's personal profile—a situation that has become all too familiar—be sure to quickly remove the post and provide an explanation for what happened. If the crisis is coming from a poor experience by a key stakeholder who has taken to social media to air their grievances, be sure to quickly engage with them and directly connect them with someone who can resolve the problem. Always make sure to follow up to ensure it was handled appropriately. Key considerations on engagement and response to social media crises will be addressed in Chapter 5.

At this point a goal has been established for the purpose of social media, which relates to the organization's main vision; each platform has a vision statement associated with it and SMART, outcome-based objectives have been created; all the brand profiles are optimized; and the brand has a content distribution model and general content calendar outlined. It is now possible to create individual social media campaigns that support the larger role of social media in an organization.

## Social Media Campaign Design

Similar to the larger social media strategic plan, each individual campaign will have similar pieces. A social media campaign allows an organization to strategically design a shorter-term engagement plan around specific topics on social media. The creation of a social media strategic plan will be the unifying and guiding parameter for all campaigns that are produced by an organization.

### *Developing Campaign Goal(s)*

As with the strategic plan, a social media campaign goal will be the broad end-purpose for the campaign. Unlike the strategic plan, however, the campaign's goal may be more short-term in nature. For example, a campaign goal might be: "Be a leading choice for summer vacation destinations." Or perhaps it might be something along the lines of: "Be a top charity to donate to and engage with during Giving Tuesday." Social media campaign goals directly relate to the organization's vision and, more specifically, to the social media strategic design goals. They are ultimately born out of the formative research collected in the listening phase. These goals may also have been identified from the SWOT analysis. For instance, an example of a SWOT application for a goal by a temp agency on social media may have been that there is significant opportunity to engage with potential new hires via LinkedIn. That opportunity relates to the vision of the organization being accomplished (finding people to fill positions) and supports the social media goals (the organization's desire to use social media as a way to take advantage of finding potential hires). As a result, it may be determined that there is a need to create a specific social media campaign that pursues this opportunity which should take place between April and June in order to target new graduates. Remember, any goal for a social media campaign should be driven by data—not just reactions. Be sure to thoroughly review all areas of research and needs for an organization prior to establishing the social media campaign goal.

### *Audiences*

After establishing a campaign goal, identify which audiences are most important to the success of this particular campaign. While an organization may have a variety of primary and secondary audiences, each campaign should be tailored to the most appropriate audience for the given goal. An

| Public | Important Segment | Profile | Priority |
|---|---|---|---|
| College Students | Freshman | Typically 17–18 years old; prefers Snapchat and Instagram as platforms; values entertainment on social channels. | Primary |
| Parents of College Students | Moms of Freshmen | Active on Pinterest and Facebook; values information on helping their students and resources for college funding. | Secondary |

*Figure 3.3* PIPP Chart for Audience Analysis

audience can be defined as: "people who are somehow mutually involved or interdependent with particular organizations" (Broom & Sha, 2013, p. 2). In this context, consider which audiences or platform communities are especially involved with the success of the given campaign goal. The audience analysis that was conducted during the listening stage is particularly helpful during this point. The analysis specifies information such as user demographics, key behaviors of certain stakeholders, and important communication background (such as other places the audience is receiving information and how often). Be sure to clearly identify the values, opinions, beliefs, and behaviors of each audience and then select those that are most related to the success of the campaign goal. Create an audience profile for each of the key publics involved in the campaign. An easy way to create this kind of audience profile is to use PIPP: Public, Important Segment, Profile, Priority (Guth & Marsh, 2012, p. 240). An example of an audience profile chart can be seen above. These audience profiles will help develop the rest of the social media campaign.

### Campaign SMART Objectives

As with the strategic plan, create SMART outcome-based objectives for the campaign. These objectives must directly support the goal created for the campaign and be related to the specific audience or platform community that was identified in the audience analysis section. For most audiences, brands may have one specific objective. However, some campaigns necessitate multiple objectives for an audience in order to achieve a goal. By first identifying the audience and having their profile developed, the SMART objectives can be much more strategic and precise. This also provides a clearer understanding of who the audience is, what they value and want from the organization, and what behaviors are typical. This information gives data to develop "achievable" and "relevant" goals that are appropriate for the campaign.

Finally, be sure each objective supports the goal. Sometimes there are some fantastic social media objectives, but they do not lead to the goal being reached. Social media strategists should consider the following question: if each of these objectives is met, does that mean the goal has succeeded? If the answer is yes, move forward with developing campaign strategies. If the answer is no, it is important to evaluate which objectives may need to be removed or refined, and whether there are additional objectives that should be added.

### Strategies

With the goal, audiences, and objectives in place, it is now possible to move into the "what" stage of planning by creating strategies to achieve those campaign objectives. Strategies are defined as the "overall concept, approach, or general plan for the program designed to achieve an objective" (Broom & Sha, 2013, p. 273), or as "how and why campaign components will achieve objectives" (Wilcox & Cameron, 2009, p. 154). Essentially, *strategies* are the ways or approach in which a campaign will effectively work toward reaching objectives. For example, a strategy might be: "Develop a photo contest to highlight the new product in use by fans." This is a concept that may lead to an objective being met. Another example could be: "Launch a quarterly Twitter chat to provide thought-leadership in education." The idea behind strategies is that they are *what* will be done as part of the campaign in order to achieve an objective. It is likely that there will be three to five strategies for each objective, though that may vary depending on the campaign and specific needs. This is where creativity starts coming to life as strategists intentionally identify the kinds of activities and initiatives that would be beneficial in the campaign and required for the success of objectives.

### Tactics

After identifying the "what" of the campaign, the various parts to accomplish those strategies, also known as tactics, are needed. *Tactics* can be defined as "the nuts and bolts part of a plan" (Wilcox & Cameron, 2009, p. 156). They are the specific activities and tasks that must be completed for a strategy to be fulfilled. List all the specific pieces and actions that need to happen in order to make a strategy successful. For example, one strategy above identified a photo contest. In order to accomplish this, many tactics must be in place. Rules must be developed. Prizes must be identified and secured. Media and posts must be created for the specific platform that is hosting the contest. Each strategy can only be accomplished if specific *tactics* take place. Just like before, at the end of making the list of tactics, consider the following: "If all of these tactics happen, will that make the strategy successful?" If so, move forward. If not, it is time to re-assess the tactics.

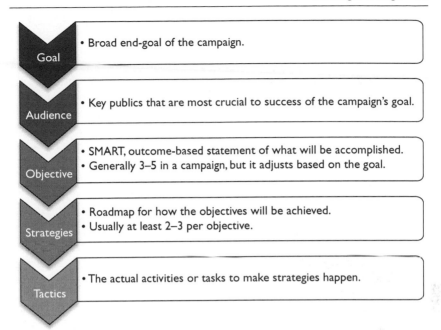

*Figure 3.4* Social Media Campaign Elements

### Key messages

To create key messages, the words and content must be based on the individual audiences to which the brand will be communicating. A *key message* is the core concept, or elevator pitch, that is used to develop other communication pieces. Think of one to two sentences that capture the heart of the campaign, designed with the brand persona, tone, and language in mind, that strategically matches the unique needs and values of the audience that the campaign is designed to reach. For example, when looking to engage new moms in relation to a product that recently launched, a key message might be: "The [new product] is a safe and effective way to help you care for your child." When developing a key message, consider the following:

- What does the audience value?
- What unique benefit does this brand, cause, product, service, or event offer in relation to the audience's need?
- Which keywords or topics capture this issue?
- What would be most important in this topic for the audience to know?
- How would our brand persona and tone strategically articulate this concept?

After crafting a key message of one to two sentences for each audience in the campaign, it is time to develop a social media message map.

## *Message Map*

A message map will guide the communications on social platforms. It can be defined as, "a framework used to create compelling, relevant messages for various audience segments and for organizational alignment" (Covey, n.d., para. 1) or a "compass that guides all of your communications" (Melcrum, n.d., para. 2). Essentially, it is a way to extrapolate how to communicate in meaningful ways with each audience. The word *communication* is a term derived from the Latin word *communis*, which means "common." This is applicable as it is common knowledge and experience that leads to connections that intertwine communities. As a message map is developed, identify the commonalities, or mutual interests, between the brand and key audiences to make the connection through communication stronger.

First, when developing a social media message map, create a guide for how to communicate the key messages in various settings. For example,

*Figure 3.5* Social Media Message Map

perhaps there will be a key message for an audience followed by several supporting, longer, messages that could be used to craft posts for various platforms like Facebook, Twitter, and LinkedIn. Keep in mind: a message map is not a copy-and-paste place to put all social content. It is a place to model how to effectively communicate the key message in the various places for the campaign.

Second, consider creating supporting messages in ways that engage a variety of kinds of people, such as articulating key messages with facts, statistics or logical points (*Logos*), using stories and anecdotes (*Pathos*), and testimonials or endorsements and success stories (*Ethos*). This will help the messages truly resonate with a variety of perspectives and brand community members. Also consider examples of how *not* to communicate the key message. This could be a secondary part of a social media message map to help provide specific guidelines and examples for ways that the brand persona or tone would not be applied to a concept.

## Budget and Resources

A final component to designing a campaign is identifying the budgetary needs and resources that will be required to accomplish the campaign. Social media is not free. It takes staff hours, money for giveaways, time to create graphics, and any number of other elements to make it successful. A social media professional should be able to identify those needs and document them for the campaign. The first step is to create a list of all resources needed. This should include things such as social media interns (if applicable), staff time, creative design, etc. Next, add a column beside each of these items and list the cost of them. This will calculate the total expenditures expected for the social media campaign. It is also important, however, to list income.

### Calculating Potential Social Media Income

While some argue that it is impossible to attribute income to social media, many businesses have found that it drives revenue in some remarkable ways. A vast majority of social media value comes in the form of developing stronger relationships, increasing the brand's credibility and engaging in two-way dialogue. However, social media strategists should be able to harmonize the return on investment both in monetary, bottom-line elements as well as in some of the intangible dimensions of social media value. This section will focus on the first type of calculation: bottom-line dollars.

In order to calculate the potential income, review the campaign objectives. Each objective has a specific and measurable outcome. Coordinate with the marketing and IT department to ascertain the value of that outcome. For example, if one of the objectives was to have 25 sign-ups for a free giveaway in the month of May, ask the marketing team for the value for each name that is collected. In the budget, identify the value per name and multiply it by the 25 potential sign-ups identified in the SMART objective to determine the potential income associated with the objective. Some social actions contribute to larger organizational objectives. For example, it could be that the value of a sign-up for the free giveaway needs to be split between the SEO team, which is optimizing the landing page for the giveaway, and the social media team, which drove traffic to the page. The social media objective, therefore, is considered a secondary or complementary driver of the bottom-line conversions. It is helpful to discuss with the marketing department and management what percentage of value can be agreed upon to attribute to the social action so a specific dollar amount can be assigned to the behavior objective in a campaign. When those values are determined, subtract the total costs from any total income that can be attached to an objective to determine the monetary value of the campaign.

It is worth noting that much of social value is found in developing healthy relationships and communication with key stakeholders, not driving bottom-line business revenue. There is strong precedent in the public relations and communication fields to establish objectives that are based on increasing credibility, developing trust, and influencing predispositions of audiences. These interactions still provide value for the organization by benefitting the continued health of relationships that are key to the organization's success. If a social media objective relates to a category that is more public relations or communications rather than marketing specific, it may be helpful to add a note at the bottom of the budget regarding the non-monetary value that will be added to the organization through relationship efforts and the implications for the success of the organization as a result.

Finally, before concluding the discussion on the elements of strong social media strategic plans and campaign designs, consideration must be given to ethics within the social media context. With the increased use of social media by organizations, a new capacity to engage and maintain two-way communication has become a norm for brands. However, these social platforms have also posed ethical concerns that include activities such as ghost blogging, responses to negative comments online, transparency by organizations, privacy issues, and coercive communication efforts (DiStaso & Bortree, 2014). The heart of social media has always been about relationships—and that is why it is crucial for organizations to develop a strong ethical framework that supports social media activities. Each social media strategic plan and campaign should be reviewed to ensure it upholds the highest ethical standards for organizations engaging in social media.

## Social Media Ethics

Organizations that use social media face a multitude of ethical questions: some that are significant and others that may seem rather small. Social media strategists need to be able to identify areas of ethical concern and apply an ethical framework to social media decision making in order to best serve their organizations and the social media community. Brian Solis explains the concept like this:

> At its very core, social media is not about technology, it's about people. Connections, emotions, expression become the souls and personalities of online communities. The ties that bind them together are relationships. Without value, mutual benefits, the quality of the relationship erodes.
>
> (DiStaso & Bortree, 2014, p. xv)

A core commitment to the well-being of the relationships developed in social media should be a primary consideration for ethics by organizations within social spaces. In order to accomplish this commitment to relationships and ethics, many suggest using the "Ethics of Care" principles when interacting in social media. This can be defined as "doing what is right using the principles of care and concern" (McCorkindale, 2014, p. 67). Walton and Stoker (2007) suggest that "The ethic of care moves beyond thinking about the relationship in terms of organizational or personal rights and places an emphasis on relationships and an organization's responsibility to relationships created under its care" ( p. 11). In other words, "the ethic of care's focus on interdependence, mutuality and reciprocity mirrors our perspective on public relations. . . . We cannot choose to ignore a relationship with a stakeholder simply because it is not important to us" (Coombs & Holladay, 2014, p. 40). *Ethics of Care* is when decisions and interactions are guided by a deep commitment to the inherent value of relationships and the responsibility to protect those relationships as the primary guide for the brand. To provide a framework to approach social media campaigns with an ethic of care, this chapter will explore several key considerations for social media strategists.

### Defining Ethics

In order to understand a proper application of ethical approaches to social media, one must first understand what is meant by the concept of ethics. Scott Rae (2009), a well-known ethicist and researcher, points out that often there is confusion between morality and ethics:

> Most people use the terms morality and ethics interchangeably. Technically, morality refers to the actual content of right and wrong,

and ethics refers to the process of determining right and wrong. In other words, morality deals with moral *knowledge* and ethics with moral reasoning. Thus, ethics is both an art and a science. It does involve some precision like the sciences, but like art, it is an inexact and sometimes intuitive discipline. Morality is the end result of ethical deliberation, the substance of right and wrong.

(p. 15)

Ethics, then, involve determining a course of proper behavior based on existing standards, not simply reactive to a tense moment in social media. Brian Solis suggests that "without a strong ethical foundation, you unintentionally make perilous decisions driven by what's right . . . right now, rather than what's truly right" (DiStaso & Bortree, 2014, p. xvi). In other words, ethics help identify right actions by what we should do and wrong actions by what we should not do (Fagothey, 1976, p. 2; Baker & Martinson, 2001, p. 155). But the question still remains as to which standards can help guide the process of determining proper behavior and inappropriate behavior. In order to address this, there are several ethical principles that social media professionals can use as they develop campaigns.

The first principle stems from the idea that ethics involves making decisions that can be justified to another person, not just to the brand. This is what Bok (1989) would call "public justification" (p. 97). Essentially, the "test of publicity" (Baker & Martinson, 2001, p. 155) involves being capable of justifying, to a reasonable audience, that the communication was ethical (Jaksa & Pritchard, 1994, p. 107). Rather than relying on the justification that can fall down an ethically slippery slope when only considering the organization's goals, social media professionals should consider every social media post through the lens of how the public would perceive the interaction. This consideration should be based in a fierce commitment to protecting and sustaining relationships, not in reaching bottom-line goals for a company. For example, ethically, organizations should disclose when employees or professionals are being paid to endorse the brand online. Otherwise, it is a deceptive practice because the social community is unaware of the financial incentive associated with the content posted.

Ethics will come into play on a daily basis—sometimes forcing social media teams to make significant decisions, and other times surfacing in the seemingly typical interactions that happen when responding to tweets, comments, and mentions. "Many decisions you will make on a day-to-day basis involve questions of right and wrong, some of which may have easy answers but are difficult to carry out. Ethics provide the basis on which you make those decisions" (Rae, 2009, p. 12). A key component to the basis for making ethical decisions in social media is understanding the goal and purpose of *social* media: relationships.

## Dialogic Communication Ethics

As previously identified, a key component to social media initiatives by organizations is to develop relationships with their online communities. While social media can be used to support overall business objectives and, at times, yields direct business profits, it often is used to support the long-term value of strong relationships with key audiences. It is helpful, therefore, to examine historical approaches to relationship building and theories that would apply to social media, in order to create an ethical schema for social media professionals.

Grunig and Hunt (1984) proposed four models for how the public relations process, or the act of building mutually beneficial relationships, has been practiced throughout history. They conclude that a two-way symmetrical model is the best approach, as it "uses research to facilitate understanding and communication rather than to identify messages most likely to motivate or persuade publics. In the symmetrical model, understanding is the principal objective of public relations rather than persuasion" (Grunig & Grunig, 1992, p. 289). The idea of mutual understanding and communication fits perfectly into the core purpose of social media. Thus, using a two-way symmetrical theory to analyze social media communication is important. In addition, using a two-way symmetrical theory to relationship building also allows for a co-creational perspective of communication, which is in line with the idea previously addressed of social media communities being composed of "prosumers" not consumers. Botan and Taylor (2004) point out "the co-creational perspective sees publics as co-creators of meaning and communication as to what makes it possible to agree to shared meanings, interpretations and goals" (pp. 651–652). Social media is uniquely designed to support this model of relationship building, being contingent on the public and organizations interacting to pursue mutual understanding by co-creating the conversation within the social environment. It is a two-way, joint dialogue around a conversation of mutual interest. The commitment to dialogue, which should be "ethical, honest, forthright, and authentic" (DiStaso, 2014, p. 36), is what gives dialogic communication ethics a foundation to be applied in social media.

*Dialogic communication* can be defined as "any negotiated exchange of ideas and opinions" (Kent & Taylor, 1998, p. 325). In other words, when organizations develop strategic plans to engage in conversation with online communities, a dialogic communication approach is being used. However, for authentic dialogic communication to occur, a two-way process must happen: online communities and organizations interacting—not just a pushing of content from organizations. Essentially, "this requires that both parties are willing to be open and listen to the other even if there is disagreement and the communication should be focused on intersubjectivity" (DiStaso, 2014, p. 34). The focus on this authentic, two-way dialogic communication should guide strategies within social media campaigns. The focus needs to remain on the conversation and relationship, not just publicity for brand messages. Kent and Taylor (1998) suggest

> for a dialogic relationship to exist, parties must view communicating with each other as the goal of a relationship. Communication should not be a means to an end, but rather, as Kant's Categorical Imperative suggested, communication should be an end in itself.
>
> (p. 322)

In order to understand what it would look like to make ethical decisions based on communication itself, rather than as a tactic to force a certain behavior, Baker and Martinson (2001) proposed a five-step process: TARES.

### The TARES Ethics Model

Baker and Martinson (2001) suggest that there are five principles that can help guide communication efforts. These five duties are: truthfulness of the message, authenticity of the organization, respect for the people being communicated with, equity of the message, and social responsibility (p. 159).

### Truthfulness of the Message

The concept of truthfulness within the TARES test incorporates a broad approach to accurate information. As previously mentioned, trust is a cornerstone of relationships. When it is harmed, the value of the relationship is diminished. Bok (1989) went so far as to describe the value of truthfulness in relationships by saying "trust is a social good to be protected" (p. 26). In other words, truthfulness in the TARES test is beyond simply sharing literal truth and goes to the heart of the idea of trust: does the information provided give transparent content, not designed to deceive, allowing individuals to make informed decisions. In an effort to further define what "transparent" messages would include, Rawlins (2009) suggests that transparent means:

> The deliberate attempt to make all legally releasable information—whether positive or negative in nature—in a manner that is accurate,

*Figure 3.6* TARES Ethical Test

timely, balanced, and unequivocal, for the purpose of enhancing the reasoning ability of publics and holding organizations accountable for their actions, policies, and practices.

(p. 75)

For communication in social media to pass the truthful principle in TARES, it must not only be accurate but also transparent, providing complete information that is capable of allowing publics to make the most informed decision and choice possible, rather than attempting to hide, remove, or limit information that may be less than positive for the organization. Bok (1989) suggested that when information is intentionally left out of communication with a public, it is a harmful act, similar to violence, against people as it inhibits their ability to make informed choices "by preventing people from adequately understanding a threatening situation, from seeing the relevant alternatives clearly, from assessing the consequences of each, and from arriving at preferences with respect to them" (p. 26). With this in view, truthful communication is more than just putting messages that are accurate into social media. It involves providing complete and transparent information that gives audiences all the information available to make an informed decision.

## Authenticity

Authenticity of the communication within an organization requires that there is a commitment to personal responsibility and a deep concern for the value of others (Golomb, 1995, p. 204; Baker & Martinson, 2001, p. 162). In other words, "the Principle of Authenticity requires persuaders to evaluate the motivations, intentions, and attitudes that drive their persuasive activities, and to act nobly" (Baker & Martinson, 2001, p. 162). In addition, the concept of authenticity requires genuineness and sincerity when interacting in the relationships. It is important to position the brand appropriately and engage in social media around topics of mutual interest, but this must come from a communication virtue that focuses on the genuine belief that the organization makes a positive contribution to the online community. While social media teams fiercely represent the organizations that they serve, they also have a deep commitment and dedication to the good of their online communities. Balancing the needs of the organization with the needs of the online community is part of being authentic.

## Respect

This principle requires that the communication and actions through social media illustrate that the brand recognizes that each community member is "worthy of dignity, that they not violate their rights, interests, and well-being for raw self-interest or purely client-serving purposes" (Baker

& Martinson, 2001, p. 163). In other words, it should be clear that the people with whom the organization has relationships are incredibly valuable, simply because they are real people. Jaksa and Pritchard (1994) argue that people "should not be treated merely as a means to an end; they are to be respected as ends in themselves. Human beings are 'beyond price'" (p. 128). This principle is a cornerstone for the TARES model as it is the motivation that informs the other tenets: the inherent dignity and value of each person.

## Equity

The concept of equity is that all parties involved in the communication will be treated fairly. The idea is to consider the other person and identify whether they are being taken advantage of or being coerced due to the form of communication. The goal is that "the interests of some are not sacrificed to the arbitrary advantages held by others" (Cahn & Markie, 1998, p. 621), such as organizations who hold a great deal of power using propaganda on social media to take advantage of a situation. Each time a strategy or tactic is designed for social media, consider whether the primary audience of the strategy or tactic is being approached with equity, being given not only accurate and truthful information, but information presented in a legitimate way that is free of coercion, scare-tactics, and sensationalism.

## Social Responsibility

The concept behind the social responsibility tenet is that organizations have a duty to the good of society at large. This means that organizations cannot ethically be promoting causes, services, products, or events that harm the common good—as that would not meet the TARES test.

The TARES model is composed of "interrelated moral safeguards" with principles that are "mutually supporting and validating" (Baker & Martinson, 2001, p. 169). As social media professionals attempt to design strategic campaigns, it is crucial that each post, tactic, strategy, and objective is reviewed through an ethical lens in order to protect the well-being of the relationships within social media and, ultimately, the good of each individual person in the social media community. Ethical decisions should be informed by remembering the core purpose of social media: to engage in conversations with real people who have incredible value just by being human.

**KEY CONCEPT SNAPSHOT**

1. Before developing social media campaigns, brands need a strategic social media plan that will be the guiding framework for all campaigns and initiatives by the brand in social media.
2. Social media is about people. Every interaction a brand has within social media should be grounded in ethical consideration for the value and worth of people.
3. When developing policies and procedures for social media, organizations should seek to build trust and inspire . . . not control.
4. Ultimately, each component of a social media campaign is developed from a strong research base and supports the overall vision of the organization's social media plan.

## Suggested Reading

Alpert, J. (2012). *The mobile marketing revolution: How your brand can have a one-to-one conversation with everyone.* New York: McGraw-Hill.

Breakenridge, D. (2012). *Social media and public relations: Eight new practices for the PR professional.* Upper Saddle River, NJ: FT Press.

DiStaso, M., & Bortree, D. (2014). *Ethical practices of social media in public relations.* New York: Routledge.

Smith, M., & Kawasaki, G. (2011). *The new relationship marketing: How to build a large, loyal, profitable network using the social web.* Hoboken, NJ: John Wiley & Sons.

## References

*Note*: All website URLs accessed on February 2, 2016.

Armstrong, P. (2011, March 10). Social media and brands – tone is key. *Memeburn*. Retrieved from: https://memeburn.com/2011/03/social-media-and-brands-tone-is-key/

Baker, S., & Martinson, D. L. (2001). The TARES Test: Five principles for ethical persuasion. *Journal of Mass Media Ethics, 16*(2–3), 148–175.

Bok, S. (1989). *Lying: Moral choice in public and private life.* New York: Vintage.

Botan, C. H., & Taylor, M. (2004). Public Relations: State of the field. *Journal of Communication, 54*(4), 645–661.

Broom, G., & Sha, B-L. (2013). *Cutlip and Center's effective public relations.* Boston: Pearson.

Cahn, S., & Markie, P. (1998). *Ethics, history, theory, and contemporary issues.* New York: Oxford University Press.

Coca-Cola. (n.d.). Social media principles. *Coca-Cola Company.* Retrieved from: www.coca-colacompany.com/stories/online-social-media-principles

Coombs, W. T., & Holladay, S. J. (2014). *It's not just PR: Public relations in society*. Malden, MA: Blackwell.

Covey, W. (n.d.). Introduction to message mapping for effective communication. *Trew Marketing*. Retrieved from: www.trewmarketing.com/smartmarketingblog/best-practices/introduction-to-message-mapping-for-effective-c

DiStaso, M. (2014). Bank of America's Facebook engagement challenges its claims of "high ethical standards." In M. DiStaso, & D. Bortree (Eds.), *Ethical practice of social media in public relations* (pp. 33–48). New York: Routledge.

DiStaso, M., & Bortree, D. (2014). *Ethical practice of social media in public relations*. New York: Routledge.

Fagothey, A. (1976). *Right and reason: Ethics in theory and practice*. St. Louis, MO: Mosby.

Golomb, J. (1995). *In search of authenticity: From Kierkegaard to Camus*. London: Routledge & Kegan Paul.

Grunig, J. E., & Grunig, L. A. (1992). What is an effective organization? In J. E. Grunig (Ed.), *Excellence in public relations and communication management: Contributions to effective organizations* (pp. 65–89). Hillsdale, NJ: Lawrence Erlbaum Associates.

Grunig, J. E., & Hunt, T. (1984). *Managing public relations*. New York: Holt, Rinehart & Winston.

Guth, D., & Marsh, C. (2012). *Public relations: A values-driven approach*. Boston: Allyn & Bacon.

Jaksa, J. A., & Pritchard, M. S. (1994). *Communication ethics: Methods of analysis*. Belmont, CA: Wadsworth.

Kent, M. L., & Taylor, M. (1998). Building dialogic relationship through the worldwide web. *Public Relations Review, 24*(3), 321–334.

Kodak. (2010). Social media tips. *Kodak.com*. Retrieved from: www.kodak.com/US/images/en/corp/aboutKodak/onlineToday/Social_Media_10_7aSP.pdf

LePage, E. (2014). How to create a social media marketing plan in 6 steps. *Hootsuite*. Retrieved from: http://blog.hootsuite.com/how-to-create-a-social-media-marketing-plan/

Mayo Clinic. (n.d.). About sharing Mayo Clinic. *Mayo Clinic*. Retrieved from: http://sharing.mayoclinic.org/about-sharing-mayo-clinic/

McCorkindale, T. (2014). Private conversations on public forums: How organizations are strategically monitoring conversations and engaging stakeholders on social media sites. In M. DiStaso, & D. Bortree (Eds.), *Ethical practice of social media in public relations* (pp. 65–81). New York: Routledge.

Melcrum. (n.d.). Developing a message map. *Melcrum.com*. Retrieved from: https://www.melcrum.com/research/engage-employees-strategy-and-change/developing-message-map

National Labor Relations Board. (2015, April 16). *Landry's Inc. and its wholly owned subsidiary Bubba Gump Shrimp Co. Restaurants, Inc. vs. Sophia Flores (Case 32-CA-118213.)* Washington DC: US.

National Labor Relations Board. (n.d.a). Interfering with employee rights (Section 7 & 8(a)(1)). *NLRB.Gov*. Retrieved from: www.nlrb.gov/rights-we-protect/whats-law/employers/interfering-employee-rights-section-7-8a1

National Labor Relations Board. (n.d.b). The NLRB and social media. *NLRB. Gov*. Retrieved from: www.nlrb.gov/news-outreach/fact-sheets/nlrb-and-social-media

Patel, N. (2015, March 20). Everything you need to know about the Google–Twitter partnership. *Search Engine Land*. Retrieved from: http://searchengineland.com/everything-need-know-google-twitter-partnership-216892

Rae, S. (2009). *Moral choices: An introduction to ethics*. Grand Rapids, MI: Zondervan.

Rawlins, B. (2009). Give the emperor a mirror: Toward developing a stakeholder measurement of organizational transparency. *Journal of Public Relations Research, 21*(1), 71–99.

Schwab, S. (2015, July 27). Finding your brand voice. *Cracker Jack Marketing*. Retrieved from: www.crackerjackmarketing.com/blog/finding-your-brand-voice

Solis, B. (2010, June 14). The social media style guide: 8 steps to creating a brand persona. *Brian Solis*. Retrieved from: www.briansolis.com/2010/06/the-social-media-style-guide-8-steps-to-creating-a-brand-persona-2/

Sorokina, O. (2014). Save time on social media: One social media profile, one mission. *Hootsuite*. Retrieved from: http://blog.hootsuite.com/the-purpose-of-each-social-media-profile/

Walton, S., & Stoker, K. (2007, Jan. 13). Corporate compassion in a time of downsizing: The role of public relations in cultivating and maintaining corporate alumni social networks. Institute for Public Relations. Retrieved from: www.instituteforpr.org/topics/corporate-compassion

Wilcox, D., & Cameron, G. (2009). *Public relations: Strategies and tactics*. Boston: Pearson/Allyn and Bacon.

# Chapter 4

# Step 2B: Strategic Design

## Designing Creative Engagement in Brand Communities

> Meaningful engagement is a delicate art of intertwining winsome words with captivating visuals into the robust science of dynamic timing and communication theory in order to ignite significant connection and relationships within social media.

In order to ignite conversations and build relationships within the brand community, social media professionals not only need to understand the process to create a data-driven campaign design, but also to apply creative strategies to the campaign. The question that needs to be asked by an organization is how they will be able to engage their social media communities in a creative way. This chapter explores some best practices and opportunities for creative engagement in social media.

As previously mentioned, tactics are the activities or specific initiatives that are used in order to reach an end goal. Wilcox and Cameron (2009) explain tactics as "the specific activities that put each strategy into operation and help to achieve the stated objective. In the public relations field, the implementation of various tactics is the most visible part of any plan" (p. 156). Broom and Sha (2013) further clarify the role of tactics by explaining that they "refer to the actual events, media and methods used to implement a strategy" (p. 273). Tactics, then, would be identified as the actions and activities of organizations or brands that focus on achieving the overall goals, objectives, and strategies of the social media campaign.

To help frame the process of developing creative engagement pieces, this chapter will first highlight some hallmark leaders in social media and the tactics that have been used to garner engagement in brand communities. But simply understanding what brands have done previously is not enough to provide a complete paradigm that organizations can use to develop creative pieces for a strategic campaign. Instead of spending a great deal of time discussing *what* has been done before, the real question should be *why* creative engagement works. What is it about certain tactics that seem to ignite conversations, grow relationships, and enhance brand communities? To understand this, the chapter will also examine the role of brand credibility in developing and implementing campaigns. Credibility is crucial in sustaining and growing relationships with key stakeholders. Understanding the intersection of credibility with creative engagement, therefore, is critical. Finally, the chapter will conclude by looking at how brands can select the best kind of strategies and tactics for their unique brand communities. Social media professionals who understand that creative tactics are not simply repeating brilliant ideas others have had, but about strategically enhancing the organization's ability to engage in vibrant relationships, will be able to truly leverage the innovative potential of social media within a campaign.

## Leaders in Creative Social Media

There are some social media vanguards that have led the way in creative social media engagement strategies. This section will examine how some of these strategies and tactics show the explosive power of social media. Below is a snapshot of just a few creative approaches brands have used in social media.

### Snapchat

A platform that is known for disappearing content, several brands have leveraged the platform's unique capabilities to support their organizational goals and resonate with their audiences.

#### #LastSelfie: Altruism

The Danish branch of the World Wildlife Foundation launched an incredibly effective campaign on Snapchat. Capitalizing on the idea that images disappear quickly on Snapchat, the campaign focused on animals that may go extinct and encouraged the online audience to take action to protect animal species. A video released as a component to the campaign explained: "In a way Snapchat is a mirror of real life. The images you see are transient, instant, unique, and yet only live for a few seconds. Just like these endangered animals" (Castillo, 2014, para. 4). The disappearing nature of content on Snapchat was the ideal platform to communicate the key message of the danger many animals face.

#### Stories: Humanized Communication and Brand Persona

Taco Bell, an early adopter of Snapchat as a platform, is an industry leader in engaging audiences with new and creative strategies. With more than 200,000 people in their online community and an estimated 80% of their followers opening Taco Bell's snaps, their campaigns provide some vanguard examples of creativity and social voice in action (Sloane, 2014).

**Marketing Land** SECTIONS

# Taco Bell Delivers Saucy Valentine's Campaign Via Snapchat

Fast food giant comes through again on Snapchat with a clever, interactive Valentine's Day campaign.

Martin Beck on February 13, 2015 at 3:22 pm

*Figure 4.1 Marketing Land's Coverage of Taco Bell's Snapchat Campaign*

Tressie Lieberman, director of social and digital marketing, shared that "One thing we're serious about is how we engage with our fans—we engage them the way they expect to be engaged. . . . We do it in a way that provides value back the audience" (as quoted by Morrison, 2014, para. 10). That value is measured by whether the audiences co-create content, watch the entire snap, repeat the story, and whether the stories show up in popular culture. Taco Bell president Brian Niccol says that is how Taco Bell identifies whether their social content is genuinely connecting with their audiences (Epstein, 2014, "Snapchat Hysteria," para. 8–10). Lieberman explains that Taco Bell's digital approach and Snapchat success is all about the personal engagement with their community. "It's all about treating them like personal friends and not consumers" (as quoted by Hunt, 2014, para. 2).

## Pinterest: Prosumers and Accessibility

Known as a top organization on Pinterest, Kraft Foods is a prime example of utilizing images and content to engage their social media community, empowering the brand community to be prosumers. Jennifer Feeley, Kraft's Associate Director of Digital Strategy and Channel Activation, explained, "Pinterest has become a powerful tool for us to garner real-time insights, mine data and influence content creation, curation and amplification" (Pinterest, n.d., "Success Stories: Kraft Foods," para. 3). Kraft's Pinterest community is quite strong with over 250,000 followers. Their success in igniting conversations has resulted not just in their own content being shared but also in the community creating and sharing content of their own around the Kraft brand.

### YouTube: Shared Values

Known for campaigns that resonate with women around the topic of beauty, Dove launched the "Choose Beautiful" campaign across all digital platforms. The video shows two doors for women to walk through, one labeled "beautiful" and the other "average." The video went on to interview women as to what led to the choice to walk through a specific door. To describe the video, Dove (2015) wrote,

> Would you describe yourself as beautiful? In our latest film Choose Beautiful, we travel to San Francisco, Shanghai, Delhi, London and Sao Paulo to prove that beauty is a choice – and the power of this choice is in your hands.

The YouTube video, which was viewed over 6.5 million times on their US channel, helped ignite a series of conversations across platforms around the concept of what it means to believe that beauty is a choice. The video and hashtag drove users to a dedicated website around this topic.

### Instagram: Brand Personality

Helping their online brand communities engage in the behind-the-scenes experiences of their brand, CBS launched the #CBSInstagramTakeover campaign where various celebrities would run the official CBS Instagram account. "One of the best ways for the audience to experience a show is through the eyes of its stars," said Chris Ender, CBS's executive vice-president of communications (as quoted by Gonzales, 2014). This kind of strategy connected the CBS Instagram community directly with the individuals they were interested in: celebrities.

## Elements of Meaningful Communication

Meaningful communication is a critical element to keep in mind throughout a campaign. After all, if the social media efforts do not effectively communicate and connect with a brand community, it does not really matter how creative or edgy it was supposed to be—it did not fulfill the objective. Social media campaigns need to be designed with people and relationships in mind. No matter what platform or campaign, there are certain common elements that are necessary in the development of creative campaign design pieces. One of the foremost skills that is important to remember is *writing*.

### Writing for Social Media

While this book is not about writing for social media and there are already a number of books dedicated to this vast topic, it is important to give it some focus due to its value in a campaign. With the fast-paced environment of social media and the ever-shrinking length of written components, the need for strong writing is sometimes overlooked. This may be because there is an illusion that the ability to craft a well-written piece is not as crucial. Nothing, however, could be further from the truth! While every platform may have certain ways to write that break all grammar rules (#TBT, for example), basic things like a spell check and grammar review are still important. But beyond these basic checks, it is important to consider *what* to write and *how* to write it.

There are several approaches that can be helpful to brands in determining what type of content to post. For example, Matt Prince (2014), the PR + Newsroom manager at Taco Bell, suggests the IFE IFE Rule, where content should minimally have two of the following qualities: Interesting, Funny, Entertaining, Intellectual, Flattering, or Embarrassing. (A point of clarification: Matt Prince identified "Embarrassing" as the humanizing type of content people can relate to and laugh with, not the kind of content that leads to loss of credibility or trust.)

Another approach that can be helpful is from Mark Schaefer (2012) who uses RITE: Relevant, Interesting, Timely, and Entertaining. It all comes down to engaging communication. Brands must understand what type of content resonates with their audience and review any posts through those filters. If the brand is posting boring, uninteresting, or irrelevant content, the community will stop interacting and the power of social media will be lost for the organization. It is all about being the kind of brand people *want* to interact with, respond to, and engage with. Writing for social media is absolutely an art that can be learned when keeping the purpose of social media in mind: relationships. Above all else, writing in social media compels brands to develop content designed for *people*—not for *publicity*.

The second element to effective communication is ensuring that the credibility, or trustworthiness and expertise, of the brand is strong in the publics' perception.

| Writing for Social Media | |
|---|---|
| **IFE IFE Policy** | **RITE Review** |
| • Interesting | • Relevant |
| • Funny | • Interesting |
| • Entertaining | • Timely |
| • Intellectual | • Entertaining |
| • Flattering | |
| • Embarrassing | |

*Figure 4.2* Approaches to Social Media Writing

## Credible Engagement

Because social media is all about relationships and common interests, credibility of a brand plays a significant role within social media engagement. *Social Credibility* is essentially the publics' perception of a brand's expertise and trustworthiness illustrated by being authentic, transparent, and truthful in communication. Mark Schaefer (2012) describes credibility as being a conduit through which social influence happens. When brands are credible in the eyes of the public, they are viewed as trustworthy experts, or authorities, in their industry. As this occurs, organizations are able to develop meaningful influence among their key publics and develop relationships within brand communities that are long-term. But the real question is, what leads to this kind of authority? How is a brand able to develop trust? If it is such a crucial part to the success of relationships between publics and brands, it needs to be a prominent area of focus for social media. This all goes back to credibility.

### History of Media Credibility

The concept of credibility has a long history within communication, marketing, and public relations. One area of interest for scholars has been source credibility, which looks at specific individuals or organizations (the source) that are delivering the information and the publics' perception of the credibility of the individual or brand (Gaziano & McGrath, 1986; Hovland & Weiss, 1951). Another dimension of credibility studied is based not on the source, but on the medium itself, through which the communication occurs. In other words, medium credibility studies examine specific platforms, such as television, newspapers, or the Internet, to understand the publics' perception of credibility (Gaziano & McGrath, 1986).

Credibility, as a concept, is composed of multiple dimensions that are perceived and evaluated by the public when interacting. Essentially, these dimensions are factors that are considered to be influential and important in developing the perception of credibility. Some dimensions that have historically been considered to compose credibility in both source and medium studies include trustworthiness, expertise, accuracy, completeness, fairness, believability, and community affiliation.

In addition to source and medium credibility and the dimensions contained within those concepts, scholars have also specifically looked at organizational credibility, particularly in corporate brands, and found that trustworthiness and expertise are especially important (Newell & Goldsmith, 2001). In examining how to develop effective campaigns in social media *for* organizations, this is particularly important to understand. Trustworthiness and expertise have long been the two hallmark pillars considered essential in credibility—applying it to the idea of organizational credibility in social media holds implications for the kinds of tactics and strategies that professionals select for campaigns. Simply put, in social media, which has a distinct focus on building relationships and two-way communication between a brand and its publics, credibility is critically tied to the effectiveness of relationship-building activities (Wilcox & Cameron, 2009, pp. 73–96).

---

## EXPERT INSIGHT

*Whitney E. Drake*

**What do you think is one hallmark competency social media professionals need to succeed?**

I believe social media professionals must be lifelong learners. Social media is constantly changing and what we know now is guaranteed to change. Whether it's social platform algorithms or what our audiences like, we must be attuned to the changing landscape. That knowledge will enable us to achieve our business objectives and bring value to marketing and communications.

**What are some tips to write well for social media? It can seem challenging to create relational text while maintaining brand standards.**

I have found in my personal experience, the ability to write solid press releases has been the most beneficial skill for social media writing. Being able to write a headline that captures people's attention, as well as the ability to express the most important concept in the first paragraph, helps you quickly write in 140 characters.

**How can a brand determine which types of social media tactics would resonate most with their audience?**

Social media is still a very shiny object for marketers; as such, sometimes we jump right into tactics before figuring out what our strategy and success look like. Asking questions first will help you determine the audience you are trying to meet and which platforms/tactics help you get there. Take the time upfront to figure out which partners you need and how you will work together to achieve mutually agreed-upon objectives and deliver integrated analytics reports.

**It can seem impossible to be a vanguard in social media creativity with so many stellar campaigns out there. Do you have a strategy to help keep authentic creativity flowing instead of falling into a pattern of repeating others' successes?**

Unfortunately we've come into a place where every marketer wants to create something that is "viral." We believe that in order to have successful campaigns you must have a solid base. You must be nimble and able to pull multiple levers in the digital space. For example when #TechnologyandStuff happened the team was online and able to reach out to the right folks. They knew there were marketing opportunities that could be pulled ahead to meet the increased conversation around the Chevy Colorado. Ultimately that base helped Chevrolet and Fleishman Hillard secure three Cannes awards.

**How can brands create a social community where the people *within* the community are engaging with each other as well as the brand?**

First we create community guidelines and then we provide content that helps engagement. Not every community is the same but listening to the community allows you to find ways to feed those consumer to consumer conversations. We look at this as brand health, if all you are doing with social media is creating a place to broadcast your message, the health of your community is probably failing.

**What's your perspective on using contests within social media as a part of a campaign?**

I really believe it depends on your audience and product. We have run contests that have been less successful than allowing our fans to name a concept car. The wonderful thing about social is we have the opportunity to test and learn rather quickly. The challenge is to keep track and use that data to help us drive better decisions in the future.

**Connect with Whitney:** @qoswhit | www.LinkedIn.com/in/ WhitneyEDrake | Draketake.com

*Whitney E. Drake is the Manager of Global Connected Customer Experience in the Social Center of Expertise and Care with General Motors*

## New Media and Credibility

As can be seen from the above discussion, historically credibility is considered in a single context, such as being a source, medium, or organization. But with the advent of new media, which seem to combine sources and platforms into a unique presentation of information to the public, Moriarty (1996) suggested credibility should be viewed as both a concept of the source *and* medium. This is especially true in today's digital media environment, particularly in the case of social media. In other words, brands are not *just* an organization or brand communicating on the platforms in social media—they are also viewed as possessing a *personality* (Aaker, 1997) or being a *source* of the communication. In the world of social media, source credibility dimensions, such as trustworthiness, affinity, and authenticity, merge with medium dimensions such as fairness, believability, and accuracy. All these dimensions play a role in the public's perception of a brand's credibility in social media, which ultimately holds the power to make or break key stakeholders' relationships with the brand.

It is pivotal, therefore, that professionals use social media to communicate in ways that enhance and support the publics' perceptions of an organization's credibility in order to maintain and build relationships with audiences. Studies have found that there are, indeed, specific approaches that can increase the quality of relationships and credibility between publics and brands, particularly in the fluid environment of social media (Aaker, 1997).

### Credible Approaches to Interaction

An organization's engagement approach, or methods used in social media, influences its perceived credibility and ultimately its ability to build trust

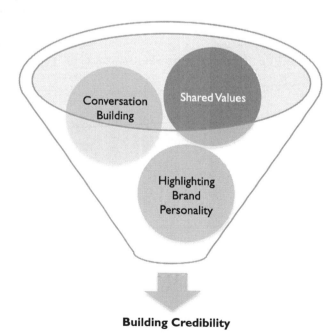

**Building Credibility**

*Figure 4.3* Methods to Building Brand Credibility

and relationships. There are three main methods that brands can use to help bolster the public's perception of their credibility: ones that highlight a brand's persona; ones that focus on conversation building; and ones that illustrate shared values. When used effectively, these three categories tend to build the credibility of an organization in the mind of brand communities.

## HIGHLIGHTING BRAND PERSONALITY

The first category of engagement includes specific actions or tactics that are designed to highlight a brand's personality. As discussed in the previous chapter, a brand's persona is particularly important in the world of social media. The concept of a brand's personality is often thought of as the "set of human characteristics associated with a brand" (Aaker, 1997, p. 347). Brands that approach social communication using this method of engagement tend to focus on enhancing the perception of their trustworthiness, expertise, and organizational reputation. These areas have a direct correlation to the personality of a brand, or the "set of human characteristics," as they are often associated with personhood or relationship.

The humanizing of the organization through this method is specifically designed to showcase a brand's personality and display the ways in which an organization is trustworthy to maintain relationships with people in the brand community. It can also demonstrate that the brand is an expert in a topic within the industry of the organization. All in all, the goal is to build the personality or reputation of the brand with the public in a positive way that encourages stakeholders to continue being active members of the brand community (Kietzmann, Hermkens, McCarthy, & Silvestre, 2011). Humanizing the brand, showcasing the brand persona and personality, allows the brand community to form a connection and feel like they truly know the brand. It helps solidify the relationships.

A great example of showcasing personality and humanizing a brand to help build credible relationships in brand communities comes from Oreo. In 2013, Oreo made social media brand history by capitalizing on the blackout during the Super Bowl. Posting a simple image of an Oreo with the words "You can still dunk in the dark," the brand received more than 15,000 retweets within 14 hours along with incredible press coverage (Harris, 2013). Since then, the brand has continued showcasing its fun personality while leveraging the power of social media across platforms. On Instagram, for example, creative photos are uploaded that highlight recipes and creative images of Oreos throughout various parts of one's day. Christopher Ratcliff (2013), Deputy Editor at Econsultancy, points out, "This policy of not taking itself too seriously and having a set rhythm of uploading a couple of Instagrams a week has led to 107,997 followers" ("Instagram," para. 4). From celebrating events such as Elvis Presley week by posting an Oreo in the shape of the head of Elvis to fun banter with brands such as Kit Kat and Taco Bell, the brand's persona and character can be felt in the images, tone, and media on any social media platform. It is warm, fun, and relaxed. This consistent approach to the brand's persona has built credibility among the brand community, making it one that is incredibly interactive.

While highlighting a brand's persona, it is also important to keep in mind that credibility is not a permanent state of being for organizations, but rather reliant on the *perceptions* of the public with which they interact (Berlo, Lemert, & Mertz, 1969). Perception truly dictates reality for brand relationships. That is why consistency is so important—perceptions can change immediately if a brand interacts in a way that seems counter to the usual brand persona or character. In light of this, it is important to consider how a brand community will perceive certain actions or behaviors in social media. Each time a brand interacts on social media, it is added to the perception of the brand's personality or character. Every post, image, video, and comment contributes to what the public believes the brand is like. As illustrated by Oreo, using social media profiles to intentionally highlight the brand persona is one approach that helps organizations connect their brand persona with the public perception of the organization. Social media platforms allow organizations to add their unique flavor to the social media environment in a professional and credible way, while also tying into existing ideas that publics have regarding what the brand should look like, based on the reputation and previous interactions they have had with the brand. Just like an individual's profile presence reveals their personality, interests, and character traits, a brand's official profile pages serve the same purpose. Be sure that the branding is consistent, and that the brand persona and personality shine through in every area of the social media profiles.

Appearance or character, however, is not the only component that needs to be considered in social media credibility. Poster (1995) suggests that social media is more similar to face-to-face interaction than mass media such as television or print publication, since social media allows for instant feedback and personal interaction. While this is true, social media also still has dimensions and characteristics similar to other media that are not present in person-to-person interactions. It is both a *source* and a *medium*. This unique blend in social media, therefore, requires consideration of not only the source, which would be the brand's persona and the organization itself, but also the medium, which would be the consumption of information through an actual social media platform. This aligns with many scholars' claims, such as Moriarty (1996), arguing that credibility is a multifaceted concept that cannot simply be confined to *either* a source *or* a medium. It is important, therefore, to understand not only what dimensions influence perceptions of credibility from sources, but also the way people perceive information through mediated communication, such as social media. This is why the second area of enhancing credibility in social media, conversation building, is so crucial. It connects the consideration of credibility not only with the source (appearance and character) but also with the medium through which communication within a social media campaign occurs.

## CONVERSATION BUILDING

This genre of engagement focuses on contributing to, interacting with, and responding to communication from publics through social media in ways that build conversations. While writing is a crucial part to meaningful communication, the *approach* to the message is also very important, particularly as it influences the perception of a brand's credibility. Four key areas to consider are engagement speed, brand accessibility, transparency, and individualized communication.

*Engagement Speed*   The first approach to conversation building that has a significant influence on a brand's credibility is the speed at which they interact and engage. Studies have identified that engagement speed is a particularly important element to brand credibility within social media due to the very nature of the platforms. Because social media is a place

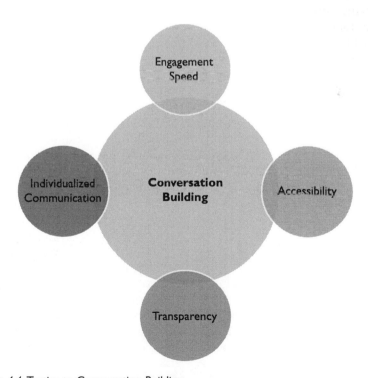

*Figure 4.4* Tactics to Conversation Building

where brand communities anticipate dialogue and engagement, the value of interaction has grown exceptionally in the eyes of the public. For example, a recent Edelman study (2013a) found that 93% of the public wanted dialogue as a key component in the relationships they had with brands. This desire is indicative of the fact that many organizations now have the capacity to have interactive communication with their publics through social media and the publics *expect* that organizations are engaging in dialogue with brand communities. When this engagement is lacking, slow, or diminished, publics may assume that the brand is either uninterested in the larger community or hiding something. This falls into line with what Scott (2011) addresses when he focuses on some changes based on the public expectation of organizational accessibility and interactivity.

The expectation of relational and interactive components to brand communication is partly why mobile marketing has been so successful— it has formed an interactive, responsive, and two-way communication between brands and publics (Alpert, 2012). The pace of social media, mobile, and digital technology has caused publics to expect brands to be swift in responding to comments, questions, or complaints, active in communicating information, and for them to invite publics into their decision making process (Edelman, 2013a; Edelman, 2013b). Brands' rapid responses and updates serve as indicators to the public that the platform is the official organizational presence on the social media sites, that information found on the social site is accurate, and that the brand community is monitored and engaged with actively by the organization (Treadaway & Smith, 2010).

*Accessibility and Prosumers*   The second method of conversation building that directly impacts a brand's credibility is the access to decision making that organizations provide for the public. Rather than functioning in the paradigm of historical approaches to marketing and public relations, Smith (2010) suggests that technology has revolutionized the way organizations need to function in today's technologically savvy, digital native world. Essentially, brands should move into the social business paradigm previously discussed. Smith's findings indicate that greater engagement with publics, more accessibility to information and decision-making, and responding to interaction in the digital world are all pivotal to the image, and, ultimately, credibility of brands. Today's public expects organizations to incorporate their feedback and allow participation in organizational decisions. Especially in the age of social media, the expectation of having an active voice in organizational decisions is growing among publics (Edelman, 2013a). It is apparent that publics are not only interested in hearing from a brand or simply being a consumer, but rather want to help produce. As prosumers, they want to have a direct say in the focus, objectives, and future of organizations or brands.

*Transparency*    The third method of conversation building, which influences a brand's credibility, is transparency in communication. Expectations of transparency have been identified as core components to the perception of the credibility of brands (Coyle, Smith, & Platt, 2012). *Transparency* in the world of social media relates to brands providing timely, accurate, complete, and fair information on a variety of organizational aspects, including fundraising structures and processes, updates on investigations and causes during crises, and details on leadership transitions, employee activity, and organizational initiatives. People anticipate that a brand will disclose information about its organization in authentic, truthful, accurate, and complete ways—and there are plenty of examples that illustrate the danger brands face when deceiving the public in social media. One hallmark example of this comes from 2009 when Honda launched a Facebook page to help highlight a new vehicle that was coming out. Eddie Okubo posted to the page talking about how much he liked the new vehicle. What was quickly discovered, however, was that Eddie was Honda's Manager of Product Planning. Since he did not disclose that he worked for Honda, but rather posted in the same way that any other member of the brand community might, the public backlash regarding the transparency of the endorsement and of Honda's social media interaction was called into question. While Honda did end up removing Eddie's post, citing that the company had an employee policy to disclose connection to Honda when posting on social media regarding Honda products, it was too little too late. The damage to Honda's credibility in the eyes of the social media community was already damaged (Kingma, 2013; O'Neill, 2009).

*Individualized Communication*    The fourth method to conversation building that strongly influences credibility in social media is individualized communication. A reality of the dynamic nature of digital communication between brands and publics is that they cannot be mechanized, or created and sent without additional interaction. Rather, social media requires interactions that are more similar to a face-to-face conversation—dynamic, responsive and unscripted (Parent, Plangger, & Bal, 2011; Kerpen, 2011). Not surprisingly, studies find that being personable through social media increases the quality of relationships and credibility between publics and organizations (Aaker, 1997; Smith, Fischer, & Yongjian, 2012; Smith, 2013; Schau, Muniz, & Arnould, 2009). In line with this, Smith and Kawasaki (2011) stress that relationships, engagement, and dialogue are essential to publics' perceptions of organizations through social media. From customizing responses for individual questions and comments to highlighting prominent individuals within key publics, organizations can utilize personal interaction, or conversation building, in order to increase relationships and build credibility with publics (Briones, Kuch, Liu, & Jin, 2011; Brown, Broderick, & Lee, 2007). While individualized interaction seems like a given, particularly on a platform designed for relationships and communication, there are many brands who have faced challenges to their credibility due to mechanizing communication. An unfortunate illustration that is often used as an example of what not to do on social media comes from Domino's Pizza in 2013 when a customer posted to Facebook about how much she enjoyed the pizza she had received. The brand's response caused quite a reaction: "So sorry about that! Please share some additional information with us at bit.ly/dpz_care and please mention reference# 1409193 so we can have this addressed" (Walsh, 2013, para. 4). While the reason for the reply was debated, one thing was clear: the meaning of communication and the authenticity of the relationship was called into question with a response that seemed pre-programmed and unrelated to the actual interaction.

While the damage to a brand through mechanized communication is significant, the power to build credibility and relationships *with* individualized messages is just as strong. A classic example of this comes from Old Spice when they launched a campaign in 2010 that capitalized on the very nature of customized engagement. Old Spice Guy Isaiah Mustafa created over 120 personalized video responses to brand community questions from Twitter, blogs, and other digital platforms in a single day. While many responses were to social influencers, enhancing the reach of the campaign, responses also were sent to general brand community members. The enthusiastic response of the campaign and the eagerness by many in the community to receive their own personal video response led to the campaign's wildly successful impact (Ehrlich, 2010; Hepburn, 2010).

Having addressed the role of brand personality and communication building, the final method to consider in building credibility is how brands and social media users share similar values. Often, these values or mutual interests are one of the strongest ties that connect organizations with their brand community.

## SHARED COMMUNITY VALUES

Illustrating how the brand community and organization have mutual interests, concern for the community, and similar values is a powerful way to build credibility. When using this method, brands must be able to authentically identify with the personal values held by key publics. These values are concepts or convictions that publics consider important. Remember the social principle from the first chapter? Social media is about those shared values or mutual interest. It is what forms the cohesive glue for tribes. Altruistic showcasing, therefore, is how the organization tangibly engages with the personal values of its publics.

In light of this, it should be no surprise that organizations that are involved in giving back to the community and actively participating in the brand community are perceived as more credible. This idea is sometimes called corporate citizenship, corporate social responsibility, or social good. While each of these terms takes on a unique approach to the method in which the brand contributes to the good of the community beyond the specific organizational objective or bottom line, they all can be categorized under the concept of altruism. A recent study found that 90% of Americans are more likely to trust and remain loyal to brands that are trying to make a positive difference by supporting causes (Cone Communications, 2013, p. 8). People want to know that the brands they care about, the organizations they support, and the social communities they are active in are committed to the same values. There are so many strong examples of brands that have led the way in illustrating shared values with the community. One common approach is to partner the brand with a cause. For example, in 2014 Toys"R"Us partnered with Shaquille O'Neal and the Toys for Tots Foundation to help provide toys to kids in need during the holiday season. When customers donated an item and took a selfie, using the hashtag #PlayItForward, Toys"R"Us would donate an additional toy to the cause. The campaign ended up raising over five million dollars (Cassinelli, 2014). But brands don't always have to partner with well-known causes and celebrities. In 2010, for example, Ford gained attention by supporting a little-known cause campaign called Invisible People, an initiative by Mark Horvath, to help with homelessness in America. By providing him with a Ford Flex and a company-promoted social site, "Ford made homelessness a primary issue on the nostalgic American road" (Livingston, 2010, "Ford Helps," para. 1). Scott Montey, former social media lead for Ford, explained the brand's support by saying, "Ford's support of the Invisible People project was never one of lead generation; it was mainly because we believed in Mark's mission and because it aligned with our own strategic initiatives." He also added, "Since the very earliest days of the company, we've always believed in giving back to the communities in which we do business—it's just in our corporate DNA" (as quoted in Livingston, 2010, "Ford Helps," para. 4).

This method of building credibility and fostering relationships in social media is widely held as one of the most powerful because it ties directly into the passions and convictions that the brand community shares. Research confirms that people trust brands that share their values (Aggarwal, 2004; Ambler, 1997). This is a concept very similar to the dimension of personal affinity that was discovered during the early years of credibility study research, which identified that people are more likely to believe in the credibility of someone they like and are attracted toward rather than someone who may be just as qualified but is less personable. Organizations who use this method to build connection and affinity within brand communities intentionally highlight the mutual areas of interest, values, and concern for the community through social media channels.

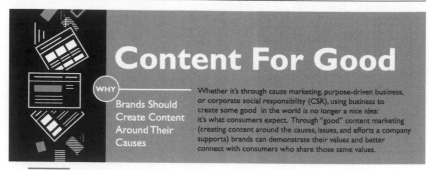

# Content For Good

**WHY**

Brands Should
Create Content
Around Their
Causes

Whether it's through cause marketing, purpose-driven business, or corporate social responsibility (CSR), using business to create some good in the world is no longer a nice idea: it's what consumers expect. Through "good" content marketing (creating content around the causes, issues, and efforts a company supports) brands can demonstrate their values and better connect with consumers who share those same values.

## Consumers Support **"Good"** Brands

Today's consumers enjoy supporting and promoting brands that support social causes they believe in.

### 90%
of Americans say they are also more likely to trust and feel loyal to companies that back social causes.

### 88%
of Americans want to hear about CSR efforts.

## Consumers Want to support Companies' CSR Efforts

**They would**

- buy a product with a social and/or environmental benefit — **88%**
- stop buying from an irresponsible or deceptive company — **88%**
- tell friends and family about a company's CSR efforts — **84%**
- donate to a charity supported by a trusted company — **79%**
- volunteer for a cause supported by a trusted company — **76%**
- voice an opinion about a company's CSR efforts — **74%**

## Why Consumers Are Moved by "Good" Content

Content marketing is most successful when it communicates a message and compels the viewer to share that same message. In a study of popular *New York Times* articles, researchers found the key to content virality is to evoke an arousing emotion, whether positive or negative.

### Probability of Making the Most-Shared List

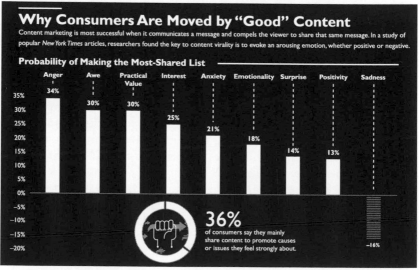

| Anger | Awe | Practical Value | Interest | Anxiety | Emotionality | Surprise | Positivity | Sadness |
|---|---|---|---|---|---|---|---|---|
| 34% | 30% | 30% | 25% | 21% | 18% | 14% | 13% | −16% |

### 36%
of consumers say they mainly share content to promote causes or issues they feel strongly about.

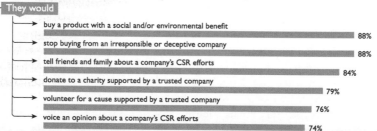

Good PR through content marketing may do more than just foster engagement. A University of California, Berkeley study analyzed Fortune 500 companies' stock prices over a 15-year period, finding that companies with a successful CSR program saw stock prices decline significantly less following a business crisis than companies in crisis without a CSR program (Minor & Morgan, 2011).

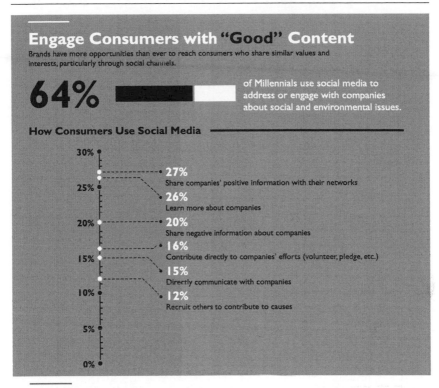

# Engage Consumers with "Good" Content

Brands have more opportunities than ever to reach consumers who share similar values and interests, particularly through social channels.

## 64%

of Millennials use social media to address or engage with companies about social and environmental issues.

### How Consumers Use Social Media

**27%**
Share companies' positive information with their networks

**26%**
Learn more about companies

**20%**
Share negative information about companies

**16%**
Contribute directly to companies' efforts (volunteer, pledge, etc.)

**15%**
Directly communicate with companies

**12%**
Recruit others to contribute to causes

# 3 Ways to Engage

**1  Share individual stories.**

Every cause has a human story. Highlighting these individual stories through content (from video interviews to individual profiles, etc.) fosters the audience's emotional connection to a cause.

**2  Show the numbers.**

Whether sharing startling statistics or showing a company initiative's success, telling the story through data can help frame information in a more understandable and impactful context.

**3  Use the Audience.**

Inviting an audience to participate by sharing personal stories or photos helps generate more content (for free!) and elevates the conversation.

A Successful content marketing strategy relies on a healthy mix of content. Creating content that triggers an emotional response helps brands do good—both for their consumers and for social causes.

**Sources:** 2013 Cone Communications Social Impact Study
Social Transmission, Emotion, and the Virality of Online Content (University of Pennsylvania)
Social Ogilvy & SurveyMonkey Study

CREATED BY

**COLUMN FIVE**

*Figure 4.5 (opposite and above)* Content for Good Infographic, used with permission of Column Five

It is very significant, however, that this method is only applied in ways that genuinely align with the values of the brand community and organization. When it seems like this method is being used by brands for personal gain, not only is the backlash quite severe, there is also permanent damage to the relationships in the brand community. Matt Petronzio, the Social Good Editor at Mashable, points out the danger of just tacking on causes to campaigns in an effort to look good: "your company needs to be genuine. Don't underestimate your consumers' intelligence by simply jumping on this bandwagon. 'Causewashing' is a serious issue, and odds are your consumers will smell it a mile away" (Petronzio, 2015, para. 5). Causewashing is a term to describe brands that attempt to appear philanthropic or to care about social good, when in reality the brand is not as authentically altruistic as it is presenting itself to be.

A prime example of the danger of appearing inauthentic in expressing shared values or community concern comes from Kmart. In 2012 the United States was shocked when 26 people, many of whom were children, were killed by a gunman in Sandy Hook Elementary School in Newton, Connecticut. Many brands took to social media to share their support and concern. Kmart, however, made a terrible misstep on Twitter when they posted, "Our thoughts and prayers are with the victims of this terrible tragedy. #PrayforNewtown #CTShooting #Fab15Toys" (Keller, 2012, para. 3). The last hashtag, #Fab15Toys, was one the brand was using as part of a campaign. The backlash from the public, claiming that the brand was using the concern for those impacted by the tragedy for self-promotion and inauthentic engagement, came quickly. One Twitter user tweeted, "An example of heinous social marketing behavior from Kmart" (Blanchard, 2012). While Kmart responded that it only used the hashtag so that the Twitter Chat participants, which ended once news of the tragedy broke, would see the support of the brand for the tragedy and not to make profit, the damage was already done. The brand community felt that rather than sharing values, and being a good corporate citizen, the organization was actually self-focused and deceptive (Keller, 2012).

Having addressed writing for social media and credible engagement methods, the third and final area to consider in designing meaningful communication is an analysis of brand positioning and creative strategies.

### Brand Positioning and Creative Strategies

Keeping in mind the many ways that interaction enhances or diminishes credibility with key audiences, social strategists should strive to develop campaigns that can enhance credibility while wielding incredible creativity and dynamic engagement within brand communities. This is definitely easier said than done.

Designing creative *and* effective tactics involves understanding the essence of the brand and positioning the organization appropriately within the brand community in order to optimize relationships. It is important to design campaigns with methods that support the overall campaign goal (discussed in the previous chapter), align with the brand's persona, and foster the publics' perception of credibility. To understand how to create tactics that accomplish this, three general approaches will be addressed: tactical methods to position the brand based on certain persona traits, tactical methods to ignite interaction in social media brand communities between users themselves, and tactics that capitalize on strategic functions of social media platforms to develop relationships.

## Positioning Based on Brand Persona

As discussed above, part of the consideration in building credibility is to position the *source* or the brand's personality as one that is trusted and an expert in the industry. The brand persona plays a critical part in knowing how to select and apply certain types of tactics within social media.

### TACTICS FOCUSING ON TRUSTWORTHINESS

Trustworthiness has been argued by some scholars to be the cornerstone for all long-term relationships. Basically, it is the most important dimension to maintaining relationships with key stakeholders. It is the life-blood of the organization. Once a brand loses trust, it can be incredibly challenging, if not impossible, to rebuild it. Because trustworthiness is so essential, strategists should regularly consider how the engagement they design in campaigns contributes or builds an organization's trustworthiness in the eyes of the brand community. *Trustworthiness* in social media means the organization using social media is perceived as honest, reliable, and possessing integrity (Morgan & Hunt, 1994, p. 23). Brent Gleeson (2012), a leadership and entrepreneur marketing journalist, points out, "Trust is the most crucial element of social media, but it's where brands continue to fall short right out of the gate" (para. 4). To develop trust, brands must recognize that they need to consistently care for, contribute to, and build the relationships within their social media communities. Key stakeholders are looking for transparency, authenticity, and honesty in organizations that also share their values and want to truly engage in two-way dialogue with them as *pro*sumers. Strategists can regularly contribute to building the trust in the brand through social media by genuinely communicating and being dedicated to the relationship in the community.

Southwest Airlines had an opportunity to illustrate their commitment to the community in 2010 when their brand came under fire on Twitter. Filmmaker Kevin Smith sent a tweet to his 1.6 million followers explaining his frustration with being removed from a flight for being overweight. Naturally, Southwest immediately experienced the fury of the Twitter world as people chastised the insensitive nature of the experience and criticized the brand (Cashmore, 2010). In the midst of this crisis, Southwest remained true to its brand's persona as a caring and relatable organization, directly reaching out to Smith, apologizing, and updating the social media community with full details on a public blog post once the situation had been addressed. While the situation was less than ideal for the brand, the response and care for individuals, time invested to personally reply to tweets, as well as public transparency in the recap of the situation led to the perception within the brand community that Southwest did truly value people, even if there was frustration with this situation.

Building trust is not something that happens overnight in brand communities. It requires time. It necessitates consistency. And it is never secure. Brands always have the potential to damage trust when they dehumanize interaction. Social media, as has been reiterated so many times before, is about people and relationships. To build trust, brands must have this as a primary commitment. Social media campaigns designed with people in mind, focusing on enhancing relationships through authenticity, creativity, and engagement, illustrate to the brand community that the organization is trustworthy.

## TACTICS FOCUSING ON BRAND EXPERTISE

In addition to the brand's persona being positioned as trustworthy, it is also important that the brand appear credible as an expert, competent in the field, and informed as an organization. For a brand to be perceived as having *expertise*, they need to possess experience or knowledge relating to the industry, and have the ability to provide unbiased and accurate information around topics of interest (Fogg, 2003; Hilligoss & Rieh, 2008). One way brands can do this is by providing thought-leadership.

When brands use tactics that focus on thought-leadership, they ultimately end up building the publics' perception of their authority as a trailblazer in the industry. Many brands benefit from using this approach within a social media campaign, as providing thought-leadership within social media is one way to also tie into a primary habit of social media users: finding and sharing news. There are a number of ways that an organization may choose to build expertise through thought-leadership. For example, using infographics in social media is a powerful way to distill a large amount of otherwise text-heavy information into a friendly and easily understandable, sharable format. People enjoy not only learning from infographics, but also sharing them with others. There are many free tools that brands can use to create an infographic, such as Piktochart, or paid subscriptions for more robust selections. Another approach might be providing white papers from the organization around various topics. If the brand is a tech organization, for example, they can consider providing a how-to guide for people on various activities they need to perform with new technology and tools. If the brand is a humanitarian organization, creating a white paper with the background and current standing of some top issues on which the organization is advocating for change is a way that it can help provide information for which its publics are looking. The goal of thought-leadership is not to position the brand as elitist and superior to those in the brand community. Rather, the focus is to provide information that the brand community cares about, may not have known about previously, and to empower them to then share that information with their friends, which will help give them social credibility as information providers too. It is a value to them to receive and also a value to them to *share*. This helps the brand by spreading awareness of topics, building trust as an authority, and ultimately being considered as a brand that provides valuable contributions to the community.

With a background in how the public perceives credibility and its connection to trustworthiness and expertise, it is easier to understand the theoretical support for developing thriving relationships in social media through two-way dialogue. When an organization only uses social media as a promotional conduit, repeatedly pushing information and product ads to users through the brand's profile, the credibility of the organization is not highlighted. Instead of looking like an authentic brand with expert insight, the organization will, at best, appear to have a fundamental misunderstanding about the nature and purpose of social media or, at worst, reflect the organization's view that the public is merely a means to an end. Social media professionals should, therefore, view the engagement opportunities through social media as a way to position the organization as a trustworthy brand with robust expertise within the industry.

### Creative Tactics to Ignite Brand Communities

In addition to positioning the brand's persona through creative tactics, social media strategists should also purposefully develop connections and conversations between the individual members of the brand community as part of a campaign's strategic design.

#### BRAND COMMUNITY RELATIONSHIPS

Social media, at the end of the day, is all about the brand community relationships. It is the shared conversations around mutual interests and values. Effective campaign design recognizes that tactics should be created to develop relationships not only between the brand and the members in the social media community, but between the individual members of the social media community. Some brands highlight the community by giving shout-outs to particularly active users during a given week, or reposting Instagram photos to the brand's account, or sharing videos created by the community while tagging the original authors. When a brand highlights the online community, it is an intentional effort by the brand to illustrate

*Figure 4.6* Brand Positioning
and Creative Tactics

| Brand Positioning and Creative Tactics | | |
|---|---|---|
| **Brand Persona** | **Ignite Connection** | **Platform Functionality** |
| • Trustworthiness | • Brand Community Relationships | • Advertising |
| • Expertise | • Prosumer Engagement | • Contests |

what others within the social community are doing on a regular basis. When creative engagement focuses on this highlighting of the community, it actually helps foster relationships *between* individual members of the brand community, as it connects and introduces people who may otherwise never have interacted. The joint interest is the brand, and the mutual connection is the content posted by the brand that highlighted an individual within the community. This developing of inter-community relationships helps the organization build stronger brand communities and can, therefore, be one of the most powerful ways to use social media.

As a result of using methods that highlight others, brands end up encouraging brand community members to engage each other more, as well as the brand. Often, these engagements will end up including comments about the brand, using campaign hashtags, or generally contributing to the share of voice that a brand has within the social world. This type of interaction in brand communities is highly significant, as studies have found that perceptions of organizations through social media are influenced not only by the brand's activity, but also by the conversations that are happening *among the publics* regarding the brand. This means that publics often are equally, if not more, influenced by peer-to-peer interaction than by brand-to-individual interaction.

What does this all mean? Essentially, when a brand's community members share positive posts, tweets, and mentions this will go far further in building the organization's credibility, and the trust of the brand in the eyes of the social media community, than any posts that the brand publishes on its own platform. These user-generated posts also help create a culture for the brand community, expanding the values, shared passion for a brand, and mutual appreciation for similar interests. A great example of this can be seen by Tough Mudder, who often creates graphics that social media users opt to use on their personal sites, share on the walls of friends, or mention other connections with in order to connect with the theme of fitness. These graphics carry messages that have a tone and approach of the brand community, rather than seeming to have the brand's official voice or message.

Knowing that members of key publics have a strong influence on each other is not something new to the public relations and marketing industry.

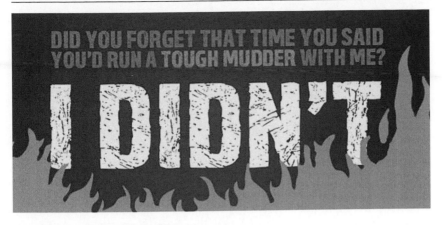

*Figure 4.7* Tough Mudder Social Media Graphic

Historically, organizations knew credibility and exposure would increase as positive word-of-mouth spread among key publics. That is why there has been so much focus on grass-roots campaigns, getting people to "tell a friend," and finding man-on-the-street endorsements for various organizations. In the social media world, this same principle applies. It is called electronic word-of-mouth (E-WOM), and through social media has taken an incredible role in shaping brand credibility. In fact, it is often suggested that in order to be highly effective, professionals should ignite conversations within social media so that others (review boards, friends, and brand community members) share the message of the organization as opposed to the organization saying it themselves. Additionally, because social media has the potential to go viral and extend to more individuals than in the case of word-of-mouth campaigns conducted in the offline world, social media E-WOM is even more significant for organizations. Because the information is coming from a peer and not the organization, it appears to be less biased, more authentic, and reliable (Brown et al., 2007; King & Hower, 2013). All of these dimensions are long-standing elements to credibility and provide the foundation for *why* so many brands try to get E-WOM tactics to be a central part of campaign design.

A social media example that has made history by using E-WOM is the ALS (Amyotrophic Lateral Sclerosis) Ice Bucket Challenge. This social media fundraising campaign went viral in 2014 and ultimately raised over 2.3 million dollars for the ALS Association (Worland, 2014). This E-WOM campaign is credited as being initiated by Pete Frates, a Boston College baseball player who was diagnosed in 2007 with ALS at the age of 27 (Freberg, 2014). In this campaign, people posted a video of themselves being drenched by a bucket full of ice-cold water. In the post they would use the hashtag #IceBucketChallenge and then tag friends, challenging them to either donate to ALS, pour an ice-bucket over their own heads, or both within a 24-hour period. Truly showing the power of E-WOM in social media, this campaign reached all kinds of people, from famous celebrities such as Bill Gates, Oprah, and Taylor Swift to over 17 million people who uploaded videos to Facebook of themselves taking the challenge (Allen, 2014; ALS Association, n.d.). These videos ended up being watched by 440 million people a total of 10 billion times (ALS Association, n.d.). This is the power of social media communities, connected together, talking about mutual interests.

## DEVELOPING PROSUMER ENGAGEMENT IN BRAND COMMUNITIES

As previously discussed, individuals in online communities want to be prosumers, not consumers. Therefore, creative campaign design should also consider how the brand can be personable, invite conversation, and foster opportunities for the brand community members to directly participate in creating content or making decisions. For brands to be personal and invite collaboration they are essentially allowing the "audience to contribute to the generation of ideas" (Foss & Griffin, 1995, p. 16). Sometimes the generation of ideas may relate to core elements of the brand, and other times the generation of ideas may involve creating content that is useful and inspiring to *others* in the brand community. Contributions and collaboration, in this sense, may involve an organization's willingness to provide the opportunity for publics to have a say in the direction and focus of the organization by including publics in the planning, launching, and evaluation of activities, products, initiatives, and goals of the organization through social media. It is important to note: this cannot be an inauthentic commitment to collaboration or inclusion—the organization has to be transparent in the level and role that consumers will genuinely have as a result of interaction through social media.

A strong example of inviting prosumers to have a say was seen in Hasbro's "Save Your Token" campaign, focusing on the popular board game Monopoly. The social media community had the opportunity to vote for which classic token should be removed from the board game and which new token should be added to an updated version of the game, released in 2013. With more than 10 million people clicking the like button on the Facebook voting page, users chose to remove the iron from the classic game and replace it with a cat (Payne & Pearson, 2013). The real value of this campaign was the fact that the social media community actively had a role in shaping the future of a brand that they loved.

Sometimes, rather than providing a direct collaboration around the brand's content or direction, collaboration involves creating ideas for others within the brand community. Again, strategists should always keep in mind that they are developing relationships *with* members of the brand community and *among* members of the brand community. A great example of this type of approach comes from Target's Christmas campaign that utilized the hashtag #MyKindOfHoliday. What stands out about this campaign is that the hashtag was not strictly about the organization or brand, but rather about a concept that the brand community could interact with and dialogue around, thereby inviting participation and interaction. This allowed users to be prosumers as they shared unique ways they approached the holidays, made meals, created gifts, and celebrated the season.

## HASHTAG CREATION

In campaigns that are designed to foster conversations among the social media world, the development of hashtags is crucial. While some people may suggest "coming up with a hashtag" for a campaign and view that as an idea in and of itself, the real art behind hashtag creation is recognizing that its power rests in the ability to enable a brand community to be participatory contributors or prosumers. Hashtags should be designed to elicit the brand communities' ideas and perspectives, driving conversations and igniting ideas. Brands should always carefully research hashtag ideas to see what other brands are using the hashtag and what kind of conversation is taking place. The beauty of building conversations in social media through creative hashtags is that this is far more powerful than simply starting conversations that are contained within a single brand's community. It is actually a method to expand conversations *beyond* the confines of a set brand community and into the connections of others as users engage with the hashtag and contribute to the conversation, reaching their friends and networks. This kind of interaction demonstrates that the organization values individuals within the community and welcomes input. That is why this type of strategic design to hashtags is more than simply a method to ignite online engagement. It generates confidence in the organization's credibility by showing that the brand genuinely cares about its publics beyond merely persuading or coercing them into certain behaviors. It shows respect for the ideas and thoughts of the brand community.

## Creative Tactics with Platform Functionality

After considering brand positioning and collaboration in the brand community when designing creative engagement, the final approach to tactic design that social media strategists should consider involves analyzing the functions or capabilities of social media platforms and determining which would be most effective in the design of a campaign.

## ADVERTISING ENGAGEMENT

Paid strategies and tactics through social advertising are key components of many campaigns that brands opt to use. In 2013, online advertising became the second largest ad medium, overtaking the long-standing medium of newspapers (Johnson, 2013, "The Internet is Now the World's Second-Largest Ad Medium"). Social advertising revenue is predicted to grow by nearly 194% to reach 15 billion dollars by 2018 (Shukairy, 2014, para. 1). While Facebook is the leading platform for social advertising, there are many other platforms that have also adopted advertising options including Twitter, Pinterest, LinkedIn, YouTube, and Instagram. The latest platform to adopt advertising, Snapchat, was rumored to charge $750,000 a day when the option first became available (Sloane, 2015). However, as of May 2015, the platform followed up with a more attainable advertising solution for brands, called Two Pennies. The focus on social advertising is indicative of the power it brings. It was found that Facebook desktop ads had 8.1 times the number of clicks and Facebook mobile ads had 9.1 times the number of clicks compared to general online advertising click-through rates (CTR) (Finn, 2014, para. 4). This is indicative of the exponential reach of paid social placement and advertising.

One of the most valuable components of social media advertising is its ability to help reach beyond a current social media community. In fact, sometimes the integration of paid efforts is crucial as the reach for brands can be organically limited due to social algorithms and community interaction. Paid tactics can often benefit brands if their focus is to expand their reach, to engage more people, and to have posts placed in locations that key audiences will see.

Thanks to the hard work done during the listening stage, brands should have a clear audience profile. Using social media advertising, brands are able to specifically pick the demographics of the audience they would like to engage with social advertisements. This is a strong way to bring more people into a community, who would otherwise likely not see the content. Organizations may target people with specific job titles via LinkedIn, or certain types of entertainment preferences on Facebook. Brands are able to target ads in a number of ways, depending on the platform.

When beginning to advertise on social media, be sure to keep focused on the ultimate reason for the campaign. Keeping this goal in mind will guide what kind of advertisements a brand should create. For example, if the goal is to drive people to a specific page on a website, with the hopes of generating leads for the sales team, review which posts have been most effective with the brand's organic (non-paid) social media tactics. Social media advertisements still hold to many of the same principles as organic posts—they should be engaging, humanized, and relational. People on social media respond to relationships. Brands may consider using higher performing posts in a paid function, as they already know the posts seem to resonate with target demographics. In fact, this is often best practice when beginning social media advertising. Find the content that has been the highest performing on the platform with which a brand wants to advertise, and use that to create engagement within the advertising tactic.

A general checklist for whether a platform will be helpful is:

1. Does the purpose statement of the platform match the goal in the advertising call to-action?
2. Do the platform's capabilities in demographic targeting allow the brand to strategically reach key audiences on the platform?
3. Will the advertising functions available on the platform contribute to the ability to reach the campaign goal and objectives?

If the answer is yes to all three questions, it is worthwhile to consider advertising on the platform.

Organizations will want to test several ads to determine which yields the highest return on investment (ROI) for paid efforts. Be sure to regularly check in with the campaign to see what is being viewed, what is being clicked, and whether those clicks are leading to conversions. Perform a lot of tests in social advertising—do not be afraid to use small budget amounts to learn which ads work best and at what times. The goal is to strategically drive activity that progresses the campaign toward success. That means a lot of measurement, adjustment, and monitoring will need to occur. Also, be sure to compile several ads so that the brand can rotate regularly. People may tune out social advertising because it is boring or they have seen it too often. The key is fresh content: rotate ads, regularly refresh paid placement, and always keep content new and interesting. Finally, always keep mobile viewing in mind. Brands creating advertising for social media must realize that they are creating it for both desktop social media and mobile platforms. With more and more users accessing social media via mobile devices, it is extremely strategic to design ads specifically for mobile access.

## CONTEST STRATEGIES

One idea that many brands use in social media is contests. While many contests are often run across platforms, it is important that a brand understands the exact rules for each social media platform before beginning a contest or sweepstakes. For example, on Facebook, organizations cannot have people share information on their personal timelines in order to enter a contest. Instagram prohibits brands from encouraging users to tag themselves in photos that they are not actually in as a way of participating in contests. Each platform has unique requirements for participating and running contests, which will be outlined on the platform's contest policy document. Before running a contest, be sure that it supports the goal of the campaign; stays true to the purpose of the platform's vision statement; and aligns with the platform's regulations regarding contests and promotions.

## Identifying Appropriate Strategies and Tactics

One of the most challenging things in social media is to identify the best tactics for an organization. Thankfully, it becomes much easier when developing strategies and tactics out of the research and campaign design, rather than in a vacuum. Sometimes organizations are eager to try a specific tactic because "it worked for others." That is never a good enough reason to decide to launch a social media tactic. Each strategy and tactic should directly relate to the objectives of the campaign and the unique audience with which the brand is engaging. Be sure to understand the audience's values, behaviors, and reasons for being in the social community before developing tactics to engage with them.

Additionally, each tactic that is created has to be true to the brand persona. Some brands have very edgy tactics. Those likely work well with their organization and resonate with their audiences. However, if a brand persona is sophisticated and elegant, an edgy tactic is likely not an approach that would be beneficial in engaging the brand community. That is why it is critical to always review the social brand voice. Consider the persona, tone, and purpose of communication. Only after appropriately aligning the audience's values with the brand's voice, is it possible to select creative and engaging strategies and tactics.

When developing each tactic, be sure to refer to the vision statement for each platform. This will ensure that each strategy and tactic aligns with the overall vision for the platform. Remember, no strategy or tactic should be created separately from a rigorous review of the social media design for the campaign. It should be informed by research and background, giving the potential for exponentially more value in the social community.

Each campaign that is designed will have unique needs. And every social media brand community should be given specialized attention as it comprises a distinctive group of members who each have different personal values and traits. No two brand communities are alike. Additionally, the brand will be communicating across multiple platforms, each with their own capabilities and purpose. It is critical, therefore, for social media strategists to refine each strategy and tactic so that it reflects the tapestry of diversity of each unique social media's platform and audience, supporting the campaign's individual goal, rather than simply modeling what every other brand is doing in social media.

## Social Media Golden Rules

In conclusion, when a brand designs strategies and tactics for a social media campaign, keep in mind the golden rules of social media.

1. *Engage with others as you would want to be engaged with*: Social media is about the community and mutual interest. It is not a place to simply promote and publicize without interacting. Mirror the type of

| 1) Engage with others as you want to be engaged with. | 2) Build a community, not a broadcast platform. | 3) Leverage the platform culture. |

*Figure 4.8* Social Media Golden Rules

engagement you would want to see from your community. Be authentic, real, and genuine. This will develop the brand's credibility, making it trustworthy and an authority in the industry.

2. *Build a community, not a broadcast platform*: The goal of social media is to contribute to the social tribe that has connected around the brand. In order to build the community, provide interesting and relevant content for the community. You should always filter the content through the lens of what is valuable to the online community, what resonates with them, and what they would find engaging.

3. *Leverage the platform culture*: Each platform is unique. There are different functions, social netiquette, and expectations within different communities. Never simply plaster the same tactic or strategy across all platforms. Rather, strategically leverage each platform to uniquely engage the culture that is present.

## KEY CONCEPT SNAPSHOT

1. Social media engagement is most powerful when it focuses on *relationships*, developing written and visual content around the values of the online brand community.

2. The methods, or tactics, that an organization uses in social media directly influence the publics' perceptions of the brand's credibility, authority, trustworthiness, and relevance.

3. Organizations should consider what qualities or traits they are focusing on illustrating via social media in order to develop the appropriate creative strategies that reach campaign objectives.

4. Creative communication tactics should be designed with expert insight into the brand, the community values, and the platform capabilities.

## Suggested Reading

Aaker, J. L., & Smith, A. (2010). *The dragonfly effect: Quick, effective, and powerful ways to use social media to drive social change.* San Francisco: Jossey-Bass.

Duhé, S. (2012). *New media and public relations.* New York: Peter Lang.

Godin, S. (2008). *Tribes: We need you to lead us.* New York: Portfolio.

Scott, D. (2011). *The new rules of marketing and PR: How to use social media, online video, mobile applications, blogs, news releases, and viral marketing to reach buyers directly.* Hoboken, NJ: John Wiley & Sons, Inc.

Treadaway, C., & Smith, M. (2010). *Facebook marketing: An hour a day.* Indianapolis: Wiley Pub.

## References

*Note:* All website URLs accessed February 2, 2016.

Aaker, J. L. (1997). Dimensions of brand personality. *Journal of Marketing,* 34(3), 347–356.

Aggarwal, P. (2004). The effects of brand relationship norms on consumer attitudes and behavior. *Journal of Consumer Research,* 31(1), 87–101.

Allen, K. (2014, Aug. 27). How the ALS Ice Bucket Challenge could change PR for nonprofits. *PR Daily.* Retrieved from: www.prdaily.com/Main/Articles/How_the_ALS_Ice_Bucket_Challenge_could_change_PR_f_17156.aspx

Alpert, J. (2012). *The mobile marketing revolution: How your brand can have a one-to-one conversation with everyone.* New York: McGraw-Hill.

ALS Association. (n.d.). ALS Ice Bucket Challenge FAQ. Retrieved from: www.alsa.org/about-us/ice-bucket-challenge-faq.html

Ambler, T. (1997). How much of brand equity is explained by trust? *Management Decision,* 35(4), 283–292.

Berlo, D. K., Lemert, J. B., & Mertz, R. J. (1969). Dimensions for evaluating the acceptability of message sources. *Public Opinion Quarterly,* 33(4), 563–576.

Blanchard, O. [Olivier Blanchard] (2012, Dec. 14). @ryanschade An example of heinous social marketing behavior from Kmart http://on.fb.me/U0RvmA ht: @cbarger cc: @armano #fab15toys [Tweet]. Retrieved from: https://twitter.com/thebrandbuilder/status/279705756369047552

Briones, R. L., Kuch, B., Liu, B. F., & Jin, Y. (2011). Keeping up with the digital age: How the American Red Cross uses social media to build relationships. *Public Relations Review.* 37(1), 37–43.

Broom, G., & Sha, B. L. (2013). *Cutlip and Center's effective public relations.* Boston: Pearson.

Brown, J., Broderick, A. J., & Lee, N. (2007). Word of mouth communication within online communities: Conceptualizing the online social network. *Journal of Interactive Marketing,* 21(3), 1–19.

Cashmore, P. (2010, Feb. 14). Southwest tweets, blogs apology to Kevin Smith. *Mashable.* Retrieved from: http://mashable.com/2010/02/14/southwest-kevin-smith/

Cassinelli, A. (2014, Dec. 31). 14 best social media campaigns of 2014. *Postano.* Retrieved from: www.postano.com/blog/14-best-social-media-campaigns-of-2014

Castillo, M. (2014, Apr. 14). WWF snaps #Lastselfie of endangered animals: Selfies just got real. *Adweek.* Retrieved from: www.adweek.com/news/advertising-branding/wwf-snaps-lastselfie-endangered-animals-157138

Cone Communications. (2013). *Social Impact Study*. Retrieved from: www.cone-comm.com/stuff/contentmgr/files/0/e3d2eec1e15e858867a5c2b1a22c4cfb/files/2013_cone_comm_social_impact_study.pdf

Coyle, J. R., Smith T., & Platt, G. (2012). I'm here to help: How companies' microblog responses to consumer problems influence brand perceptions. *Journal of Research in Interactive Marketing*, 6(1), 27–41.

Dove United States YouTube Channel (2015, Apr. 7). *Dove choose beautiful | Women all over the world make a choice*. Retrieved from: www.youtube.com/watch?v=7DdM-4siaQw

Edelman. (2013a). *Brandshare*. Retrieved from: www.edelman.com/insights/intellectual-property/brandshare/

Edelman. (2013b). *2013 Edelman Trust Barometer*. Retrieved from: www.edelman.com/insights/intellectual-property/trust-2013/

Ehrlich, B. (2010, July 13). The Old Spice Guy now making custom videos for fans via social media. *Mashable*. Retrieved from: http://mashable.com/2010/07/13/old-spice-gu/

Epstein, E. (2014, May 29). Why Taco Bell went loco for Snapchat. *Mashable*. Retrieved from: http://mashable.com/2014/05/29/taco-bell-marketing-strategy/

Finn, G. (2014, July 19). Study: Mobile makes up only 6.51% of retargeted news feed ads, yet drives 8.25% of clicks. *Marketing Land*. Retrieved from: http://marketingland.com/study-mobile-makes-6-51-retargeted-news-feed-ads-yet-drives-8-25-clicks-93283

Fogg, B. J. (2003). *Persuasive technology: Using computers to change what we think and do*. Boston: Morgan Kaufmann.

Foss, S., & Griffin, C. (1995). Beyond persuasion: A proposal for an invitational rhetoric. *Communication Monographs*, 62(1), 2–18.

Freberg, K. (2014, Aug. 22). Power of storytelling and viral fundraising: Exploring the ALS #IceBucketChallenge case. *KarenFreberg.com*. Retrieved from: http://karenfreberg.com/blog/power-of-storytelling-viral-fundrasing-exploring-the-als-icebucketchallenge-case/

Gaziano, C., & McGrath, K. (1986). Measuring the concept of credibility. *Journalism Quarterly*, 63(3), 451–462.

Gleeson, B. (2012, Oct. 31). 6 ways brands build trust through social media. *Forbes*. Retrieved from: www.forbes.com/sites/brentgleeson/2012/10/31/6-ways-brands-build-trust-through-social-media/

Gonzalez, S. (2014, Oct. 24). CBS harnesses star power for Instagram 'takeover.' *Mashable*. Retrieved from: http://mashable.com/2014/10/24/cbs-instagram-takeover/

Harris, R. (2013, July 29). Eight great examples of agile marketing from Oreo. *Econsultancy*. Retrieved from: https://econsultancy.com/blog/63140-eight-great-examples-of-agile-marketing-from-oreo

Hepburn, A. (2010, July 14). Old Spice sends personal Twitter video replies. *Digital Buzz Blog*. Retrieved from: www.digitalbuzzblog.com/old-spice-twitter-social-video-replies/

Hilligoss, B., & Rieh, S. Y. (2008). Developing a unifying framework of credibility assessment: Construct, heuristics, and interaction in context. *Information Processing and Management*, 44(4), 1467–1484.

Hovland, C., & Weiss, W. (1951). The influence of source credibility on communication effectiveness. *Public Opinion Quarterly*, 15(4), 635–650.

Hunt, T. (2014, Jan. 17). The 5 best snapchat campaigns. *Postano*. Retrieved from: www.postano.com/blog/the-5-best-snapchat-campaigns

Johnson, B. (2013, Dec. 8). 10 things you should know about the global ad market. *Adage.com*. Retrieved from: http://adage.com/article/global-news/10-things-global-ad-market/245572/?utm_source=Webbiquity.com

Keller, J. (2012, Dec. 14). Kmart's Connecticut-shooting Twitter fail. *Bloomberg Business*. Retrieved from: www.bloomberg.com/bw/articles/2012-12-14/kmarts-connecticut-shooting-twitter-fail

Kerpen, D. (2011). *Likeable social media: How to delight your customers, create an irresistible brand, and be generally amazing on Facebook (& other social networks)*. New York: McGraw-Hill.

Kietzmann, J. H., Hermkens, K., McCarthy, I. P., & Silvestre, B. S. (2011). Social media? Get serious! Understanding the functional building blocks of social media. *Business Horizons, 54*(3), 241–251.

King, B., & Hower, M. (2013, Feb. 12). Consumers more likely to trust peers, experts than companies, Edelman says. Retrieved from: http://www.sustainablebrands.com/news_and_views/leadership/consumers-more-likely-trust-peers-experts-companies-edelman-says

Kingma, G. (2013, Nov. 21). Why transparency is important on social media. *Canadian Marketing Association*. Retrieved from: www.the-cma.org/about/blog/why-transparency-is-important-on-social-media

Livingston, G. (2010, Feb. 18). 5 winning corporate social good campaigns. *Mashable*. Retrieved from: http://mashable.com/2010/02/18/corporate-social-good-campaigns/

Morgan, R. M., & Hunt, S. D. (1994). The commitment trust theory of relationship marketing. *Journal of Marketing, 58*, 20–38.

Moriarty, S. E. (1996). The circle of synergy: Theoretical perspectives and an evolving IMC agenda. In E. Thorson, & J. Moore (Eds.), *Integrated communications: Synergy of persuasive voices* (pp. 333–354). Mahwah, NJ: Lawrence Erlbaum Associates, Inc.

Morrison, M. (2014, Apr. 13). Snapchat 'live film' introduces Taco Bell's next Locos Taco. *Advertising Age*. Retrieved from: http://adage.com/article/news/snapchat-live-film-introduces-taco-bell-s-locos-taco/292629/

Newell, S. J., & Goldsmith, R. E. (2001). The development of a scale to measure perceived corporate credibility. *Journal of Business Research, 52*(3), 235–247.

O'Neill, N. (2009, Sept. 4). When Facebook fans turn ugly: Examining the Honda Crosstour Page. *Adweek Social Times*. Retrieved from: www.adweek.com/socialtimes/when-facebook-fans-turn-ugly-examining-the-honda-accord-crosstour-page/310733

Parent, M., Plangger, K., & Bal, A. (2011). The new WTP: Willingness to Participate. *Business Horizons, 54*(3), 219–229.

Payne, E., & Pearson, M. (2013, Feb. 6). Out with the iron, in with the cat: Monopoly has a new token. *CNN*. Retrieved from: www.cnn.com/2013/02/06/living/monopoly-new-token/

Petronzio, M. (2015, Jan. 11). 90% of Americans more likely to trust brands that back social causes. *Mashable*. Retrieved from: http://mashable.com/2015/01/11/corporate-social-causes/

Pinterest. (n.d.). Success stories: Kraft Foods. *Pinterest Business*. Retrieved from: https://business.pinterest.com/en/success-stories/kraft-foods

Poster, N. (1995). *The second media age*. Cambridge, UK/Cambridge, MA: Polity Press/Blackwell.

Prince, M. (2014, Jan. 27). How to: Get a job without a resume. *MattPrince.Me*. Retrieved from: http://mattprince.me/defining-your-personal-brand/

Ratcliff, C. (2013, Dec. 2). How Oreo owns social media through Twitter, Instagram, Vine and Pinterest. *Econsultancy*. Retrieved from: https://econsultancy.com/blog/63908-how-oreo-owns-social-media-through-twitter-instagram-vine-and-pinterest/

Schaefer, M. (2012). *Return on influence: The revolutionary power of Klout, social scoring, and influence marketing*. New York: McGraw-Hill.

Schau, H. J., Muniz, A. M., & Arnould, E. (2009). How brand community practices create value. *Journal of Marketing, 73*(5), 30–51.

Scott, D. (2011). *The new rules of marketing and PR: How to use social media, online video, mobile applications, blogs, news releases, and viral marketing to reach buyers directly*. Hoboken, NJ: John Wiley & Sons, Inc.

Shukairy, A. (2014, Dec. 6). Social media ad spending: Statistics and trends [infographic]. *Invesp*. Retrieved from: www.invesp.com/blog/social-media-ad-spending/

Sloane, G. (2014, Aug. 22). Snapchat's 'crazy engaged' users can't resist a message from Taco Bell: Brands see success despite marketing in the dark. *Adweek*. Retrieved from: www.adweek.com/news/technology/snapchats-crazy-engaged-users-cant-resist-message-taco-bell-159677

Sloane, G. (2015, Jan. 14). Snapchat is asking brands for $750,000 to advertise and won't budge. *Adweek*. Retrieved from: www.adweek.com/news/technology/snapchat-asks-brands-750000-advertise-and-wont-budge-162359

Smith, B. G. (2010). Socially distributing public relations: Twitter, Haiti, and interactivity in social media. *Public Relations Review, 36*(4), 329–335.

Smith, C. (2013, July 19). 10 social media statistics that should shape your social strategy. Retrieved from: www.businessinsider.com/strategic-social-media-statistics-2013-7

Smith, M., & Kawasaki, G. (2011). *The new relationship marketing: How to build a large, loyal, profitable network using the social web*. Hoboken, NJ: John Wiley & Sons.

Smith, A. N., Fischer, E., & Yongjian, C. (2012). How does brand-related user-generated content differ across YouTube, Facebook and Twitter? *Journal of Interactive Marketing, 26*(2), 102–113.

Treadaway, C., & Smith, M. (2010). *Facebook marketing: An hour a day*. Indianapolis: Wiley Pub.

Walsh, M. (2013, Aug. 13). Domino's pizza is so used to apologizing it begs pardon from fan for 'best pizza ever.' *NY Daily News*. Retrieved from: www.nydailynews.com/news/national/domino-pizza-accidentally-apologizes-fan-article-1.1425564

Wilcox, D., & Cameron, G. (2009). *Public relations: Strategies and tactics*. Boston: Pearson/Allyn and Bacon.

Worland, J. (2014, Aug. 11). Here's how much money the ALS ice-water stunt has collected. *Time*. Retrieved from: http://time.com/3101166/als-ice-bucket-challenge-fundraising/

# Chapter 5

# Step 3: Implementation and Monitoring

## Joining Conversations and Creating Purposeful Interaction

> Strategic campaigns recognize that brands must engage and build meaningful conversations within social spaces to truly be effective in leveraging the potential of social media platforms.

Having completed the first two steps in developing a social media campaign—formative research in social listening, and strategic design in campaign creation—it is now time to implement the campaign. This is the most visible part of any social media effort. Sometimes, in an effort to stay relevant and be engaged, brands jump straight into this stage. They neglect the listening that helps identify which conversations and people are most relevant in their social communities, and the strategy to ensure their social efforts support organizational goals. Both of those steps are essential in order to effectively implement a social campaign and develop robust engagement with social media communities. This chapter will explore two general areas: 1) implementing content through the use of a content calendar, and 2) monitoring the impact of the campaign using constant engagement with social communities.

### Content Calendars

A content calendar, as previously described in the general content calendar portion of a strategic plan for social media, helps develop purposeful interaction across all the platforms on which a brand is active. The goal of a campaign content calendar is to capture all the information that is needed in order to implement the campaign effectively, requiring it to have much more detail compared to the general social media content calendar. In addition, because it is a holistic calendar, it gives a "big picture" perspective of the communication occurring across all platforms, allowing a unified approach to engagement with online audiences. Put simply, *content calendars* are documents that contain each post and all content that is to be posted in a given time-period, for all platforms, and identify the way in which those posts support the campaign objectives.

*Figure 5.1* Content Calendar Elements

## Key Elements

There are several key components that should be present in a social media campaign content calendar. The areas to specify include: the date, platform, organizational objective being supported, specific campaign goal/ objectives being supported, precise audience the message is created to reach, strategy that is being enacted, keywords or topic of the content, the action desired from the audience as a result of the content, and the actual content of each post. The ideal process is to create a content calendar for the entire campaign while also leaving flexibility for some adjustments to be made in real-time. While the content calendar will document the campaign delivery, it will not be able to capture the ways to respond to a social community, which is a key component of a social campaign. This real-time interaction behavior will be addressed later in this chapter. At this point, a social media campaign content calendar should simply be able to effectively reflect each strategy and tactic that was identified in the campaign design.

### Meaning Making

A primary goal of developing a content calendar is that specific attention is given to understanding *when* it will be most meaningful to deliver a message to a particular audience (Wilcox & Cameron, 2009, p. 156). As part of this, review the information gathered during the listening stage in order to identify the best days and times to engage on platforms with specific audiences. While it is possible to find general information such as this online, it is always beneficial to compare those general studies to the research gathered on the specific social media community of the individual brand that the campaign is designed to engage. Next, consider whether there are any significant events or dates that are occurring during a campaign that should be kept in mind. Be sure to leverage certain holidays or events to enhance a message. For example, a non-profit brand may encourage giving of donations during Thanksgiving or Christmas, tying in to the general cultural communication of benevolent actions in the holiday season. Another area to identify is dates that the organization would want to avoid posting on, or develop a post specifically dedicated to the date apart from any campaign messaging in order to show respect, such as 9/11. Keeping in mind the social media community's engagement times and general events in the year, social media strategists are able to develop a holistic social media campaign calendar.

### Integrating a Content Distribution Plan

Previously, a content distribution plan was created that identified the percentages of social media posts that would be dedicated to specific organizational objectives. It is important to reference this plan when developing a social media campaign content calendar. This will aid in designing posts that not only stay in line with the organizational goals, but also specifically support the campaign's objectives. For example, a brand may still end up with 45% of the posts driving traffic to the website, but now the traffic will be driven to the specific landing page that is the focus of the social media campaign, as opposed to the homepage that may have been the generic link used for social media posts not associated with the specific campaign.

Also identify whether any other, non-campaign-specific social media content will be posted during the life-cycle of the campaign. To determine if this is the case, look at the general social media calendar for the department. It may be that on LinkedIn, every Friday there is a workplace tip for employees. That would be something to keep in mind when developing posts for the social media campaign content calendar. If, as part of the campaign, a change to that post topic needs to take place, that should be addressed with the social media director as well as the HR team, who would need to be notified so they are not caught off guard when the Friday work-place tip content is not posted during the campaign. However, it may also be possible to maintain certain generic posts while customizing them for the genre of the campaign. If a social media campaign is focused on the ways the organization can enhance leadership training, for example, the Friday post for employees could be customized to describe how managers can effectively develop leaders in their departments. This would still stay on message with the campaign goal but also resonate with the Friday focus on employees from HR.

### Campaign Goals and Audiences

The next aspect to identify is which specific campaign goals or objectives are being supported by the post. For every post, on every platform, the ultimate purpose of the post within the big picture of the campaign should be clear. Be able to connect each post to a specific goal or objective to measure effectiveness. In addition, the audience of each post should be clear. It could be that, for the campaign overall, the audience is the entire platform's users. Each post, however, may have segmented audiences to allow for stronger messaging. For example, if the organization is a university, the campaign may be specifically around recruitment. Audiences could include prospective students, parents, and incoming students. As the content calendar is created, identifying which audience is the focus of each post will help in the assessment of the campaign's message effectiveness.

## Strategy

Within this section, identify the exact strategy to which the post will relate. For example, if an advertising initiative was included in the campaign design strategies, be sure that each ad that is created and posted is labeled "advertising campaign." If a contest was launched on Instagram as a strategy, label posts that have content for the contest as "Instagram contest." As with the identification of the objectives, this will be a key way to assess effectiveness later on.

## Message Creation through Topics and Keywords

Part of a social strategy is consistently optimizing social media posts so users who are interested in the same topic can easily find them. When designing a content calendar, reference the main keywords or topics identified in the listening stage. Classify every post by a specific topic or keyword that is being focused on so it is easy to recognize which type of content posts have been effective, which categories of keywords may need more posts, and which genres of content may need to have more strategic messaging in order to be effective.

## Audience Response

Each post is tied to a specific outcome desired from the audience. Remember, every post supports a SMART, outcome-based objective, or something that the audience will *do* as a result of campaign activity. And each objective is tied to key audiences in order for it to be successful. To determine what audience response is needed for the post, consider what has to happen for the objective of that post to be reached. Perhaps it is sharing content, maybe it is clicking a link and signing up for something, or perhaps it is as simple as hitting the like button. Be sure to carefully reflect on the specific action that the audience needs to take to help fulfill the objective that the post was designed to support within the campaign.

## Content

Finally, the last portion is the actual content of the post. Within this portion it is important to reference the brand's social voice, key messages, and message map. This is the area where social strategists actually design and craft the messages for what will go on each platform for each post. Include the exact wording for every tweet, post, snap, pin, vine, and video. Be sure the wording reflects the topic, is consistent with the brand's persona and tone, resonates with the target audience, and is appropriate in length for the platform. Also include any hashtags, tags, mentions, or other elements that should be part of the post. Finally, be sure to also place the exact image, video, or link needed as part of the post. Within this content section, review the post to ensure that every strategy, such as the launch of a social media advertising campaign, the initiation of a contest, or any other effort, is accounted for within the calendar. Be sure that all details and information that need to be communicated are contained within the content calendar. The purpose is that the content section is a complete package of all the information one would need in order to implement the entire campaign.

## Review

As the content calendar is finalized, review it several times to ensure that it is on-message, supports the overall organization's communication, and is strategic for each audience. There are several steps to accomplish this review.

First, connect with the marketing or PR department to review the overall communication from the organization that will be happening via the website, blog, newsletter, or in-person to ensure that the social media content calendar will not conflict with the timing of other communication from the brand. Ideally, not only will it not conflict but the overall organizational messages will be *enhanced* as social media is used to support the mission of the brand.

Second, sort the content calendar by each platform. Review the content to make sure that multiple posts were not scheduled too frequently on any platform, that they are varied in content, and that the timing seems appropriate in light of any holidays, events, or activities that happen during the campaign.

Third, sort the content calendar by strategies. Be sure that every tactic is represented in the content calendar in order to accomplish the strategy that is being reviewed. For example, if the brand is running a contest, is there a post that introduces the contest and shares the rules? If there is a strategy that is about highlighting information and positioning the brand as a thought-leader, are there enough posts to actually position the organization as a *leader* versus something that only happens once or twice over the course of a campaign?

Fourth, sort the content calendar by topics/keywords. Review each post to make sure that the messaging is consistent. Be sure that the tone is engaging and relational, but also that the keyword or topic is clear within the message.

Finally, sort the content calendar by goals/objectives. Review the posts and ask: if the audience engages as intended with this post, will the goal or objective be met? If the answer is yes, it is time to move on to the next step in the campaign. If the answer is no, it is important to review the content calendar, identify any holes, and create the appropriate content.

A word of caution: people generally assume creating a content calendar will be quick. This could not be further from the truth. A well-thought-out,

| Date | Platform | Campaign Goal | Objective | Purpose | Audience | Strategy | Keyword/Topic | Content of Post |
|------|----------|---------------|-----------|---------|----------|----------|---------------|-----------------|
| **May 2** | Facebook | Goal #1 | Objective #2 | Newsletter Sign-ups | Young Professionals | Providing Free Resumé Tips | Resumé, Career, Young Professional | "3 tips to make your resumé stand out to managers. Sign up for a full resumé-reviewcheck-list today." PHOTO: Job Interview Candidate |

*Figure 5.2* Content Calendar Example

strategic content calendar is quite robust. It requires a lot of work and expertise to craft an effective content calendar. Be sure to allow enough time between designing the campaign and the deadline for when the campaign must go live in order to create an excellent content calendar. Effective content calendars can be one of the most important tools throughout a campaign.

## Engaging During a Campaign

The actual *launching* of a social media campaign is only the beginning of what social media strategists need to focus on during the live portion of a campaign. Throughout the course of a campaign, brands should engage with their social media communities and continually monitor their progress toward the SMART, outcome-based campaign objectives.

### Responding and Engaging

Part of dedicating time to social media as a brand is recognizing that it is not a one-way platform but rather a dynamic conversation, which requires continual interaction. To foster relationships with the social media brand community, organizations need to be available and approachable. In light of this, whether the organization only has a few hours a week or an entire staff dedicated to social media, planning time for engagement with the social media community is crucial. There are several approaches to monitoring and engaging social media brand communities during a campaign that are helpful to consider.

#### Using Alerts

Social media platforms have the option to set up alerts when something happens on a brand's profile. For example, it is possible to receive a notification if someone mentions the brand on Twitter or if someone posts to the brand's Facebook page. Whoever is responsible on the social media team for engagement on a specific platform should customize the notifications so he or she is alerted when the community interacts. This is a quick and easy way to become aware of someone engaging with the brand online. Once an alert is received, be sure to respond. Remember, studies indicate that most people anticipate that a brand will respond within one hour (Baer, n.d.).

#### Listening Principles

While responding to notifications is a minimum requirement for brands that desire a strong social media community, there are many more ways that are important to incorporate if there is the capacity within an organization. To begin with, it is helpful to implement the same paradigm as was used in the listening phase. Utilize social listening tools to monitor keywords and topics that are relevant to the brand. Also review social sites for common misspellings of the brand name just in case some mentions or comments may be missing from the official platform alerts. Dedicate time each day to respond to these topics, even if the brand has not been directly tagged or mentioned. Be sure to interact in a natural, appropriate way. Remember that social media is about being relational—not being awkward and intruding on conversations that are not highly applicable or open to interaction from the brand.

In addition to engaging the general conversations, interact with the specific content being shared as part of the organization's social channels. If the brand is gaining new followers as a result of the campaign, be sure to thank them for following. If there are people who are commenting on an Instagram picture, be sure to respond. Social media is about being *social*. A campaign will not succeed, even with the best-designed content calendar, if there is no engagement with the brand's social communities once the initial post goes live.

### Monitoring

Hand-in-hand with the launching of the content calendar on social media and engagement with the brand communities, the brand must also be proactive in monitoring the social media communication. Rather than simply waiting to evaluate the effectiveness of a social media campaign until the very end, it is important to continually analyze the responses and interaction that is being gained as a result of the campaign. Ann Handley and C.C. Chapman (2012) suggest, "Good content always has an objective; it's created with intent. It therefore carries triggers to action" (p. 15). The idea behind this is that each post created and used in the campaign has a purpose—and social media professionals should be able to watch the brand community and see whether an action has been triggered as a result of the social media post.

### Real-Time Marketing (RTM)

Along with social media content calendars and strategic planning for engagement, brands must be prepared to facilitate real-time communication. Chris Kerns (2014) defines real-time marketing as "the practice of creating content inspired by a current topic, trend or event" (p. 15). Essentially, it is the ability of an organization to adjust and participate in conversations organically, as they emerge in real-time. While it can be tempting to just stick with programmed content, the ability of a brand to adjust within the moment is crucial. That's why monitoring is so essential in social media campaigns. Kerns (2014) points out, "if the brand wants to participate in the conversation, they'll need to create a memorable take on that current event and not just try to start a separate dialogue" (p. 29). The ability to strategically design a campaign and also have expert insight into when and how to adjust and change content in light of current events is a sign of true expertise in social media.

### Planning for the Unplanned

Brands should be aware that there will always be unplanned elements during the life-cycle of a social media campaign. By recognizing significant events such as the Super Bowl, the Golden Globes, or an election, the brand can create some general content that acknowledges key components to those events. With research that is done ahead of time, pre-made posts can be crafted regarding certain elements such as the start time of the game, or the background on a candidate. In addition, planning can be done by pulling data on the conversations from the past years when an event occurred and identifying information such as: what kinds of posts were most successful? What share of voice did each group have during the event? Be sure to gather information beyond just the event itself and explore the implications for social interaction that occurred, such as which kinds of posts generated the highest engagement or involved influencers the most.

Once you have the background information from social media and the base-level details for the event, it is important to remember that real-time engagement is powerful precisely because it is not something that can be pre-made. Dynamic connection happens when a brand engages in real-time social conversations—it's authentic, in-the-moment and relevant. For example, responding to a touchdown play and tweeting the moment it happens is one way a brand could engage with real-time activity. As discussed previously, it can be hard to have the capabilities to perform with such live engagement because it requires the social team to be thoroughly familiar with the brand's voice, ready to engage in the moment, and possess the authority by the organization to not have to run a post through multiple layers of approval before going live. Essentially, real-time engagement is when social media becomes most like a face-to-face interaction with the brand: it should be informed and represent the organization well, but be deeply humanized, interactive, and relevant to the conversation at hand. It is a fluid dialogue that captures the attention of the key audiences involved in the conversation. Kerns (2014) summarized this nicely when he said,

> Uncertainty is part of the social media world, and with RTM it's no different. When you know an event is coming, but can't be sure of all the details, it takes a unique approach and a large dose of patience.
> (p. 127)

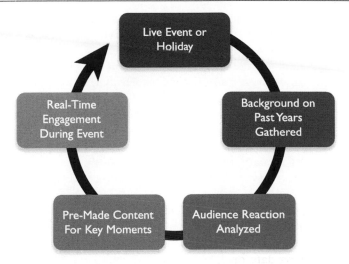

*Figure 5.3* Process for Real-Time Engagement

In addition to events for real-time marketing, brands have the opportunity to provide live engagement around questions, issues, and concerns. By monitoring hashtags, reviewing posts for any feedback or comments, and generally tracking conversations, organizations can identify and respond to relevant topics that their brand communities care about. When brands take the time to respond in real-time to interaction by the public, it illustrates the authenticity of the brand. Mark Schaefer (2012) highlighted the value for organizations that do this when he said:

> Being authentically helpful and giving of your time and talent without an expectation for reward can have a multiplier effect as your goodwill is observed and noted by others. Combined with great content and an engaged network, it is probably the single most powerful creator of connection and influence on the web.

(p. 61)

While part of being helpful and giving as a brand could include providing free resources and how-to guides, being engaged with publics in real-time, providing answers, suggestions, and helpful feedback illustrates the value of the organization and the respect for the relationships that are in social media.

### Key Metrics

In order to track triggering actions and social activity, carefully monitor each social post throughout a campaign. An effective way to do this is to use the same file that was designed for the content calendar with the addition of a few new columns: key progress indicators (KPIs), influencers engaged, and time decay. Each of these new columns will come in as very useful in step four, when evaluating the effectiveness of the campaign.

First, recording any social media engagement or actions that serve as key progress indicators for a brand helps identify that movement toward the success of an objective. *Key progress indicators* (KPIs) are metrics that provide meaningful insight into the advancement of a campaign in reaching goals. For example, the brand might record the following as KPIs for a given post in social media: 100 retweets, 340 favorites, and 25 replies. If the post being monitored is one from Instagram, it would be important to record how many likes, comments, and mentions were garnered. Whatever metrics happened as a result of a post in a given platform would be recorded in this new KPI column on the content calendar.

Second, identify the influencers that are engaged. While everyone plays a valuable role in a social media community, social influencers carry a certain level of impact whenever they engage with social content. In the listening stage, influencers for the brand and various platforms were identified. It is helpful to record whether these influencers engaged with a specific post, what they did with the post, and the result of their engagement. For example, a brand might note that a specific influencer shared a post on LinkedIn, which resulted in 100 more likes, 20 shares, and a conversation that had 15 people participating on the influencer's LinkedIn profile.

Third, identify the time-decay of the post. Depending on the detail of the organization it might be best to list the total of social activities that took place on the first day, the second day, the third day, and by the end of the first week. If it is helpful to have more detail, and time allows, record the first day's activity by hours or hour blocks in order to provide details on when the community most engaged with the content and what kind of activities happened throughout the lifetime of the post. Because the time-decay area can be quite complex, consider breaking this portion into multiple columns so that it is easier to sort later on, labeling each column either by a day or time-block period.

At the end of this stage, review the brand's monitoring metrics to assess the impact of each post, strategy, objective, and goal. It is now possible to mine this data for the most effective times to engage with audiences and ways to increase interaction with influencers. More details of how to use this information during the evaluation of a campaign will be provided in the next chapter. However, before moving on to evaluation, a crucial part of engaging and monitoring in social media is understanding how to handle a crisis while it unfolds in social media.

## EXPERT INSIGHT

*Kirsten Bailey*

**What do you think is one hallmark competency social media professionals need to succeed?**

In my opinion, the hallmark competency can be encompassed as: #ABL, Always Be Learning. The social media landscape continues to rapidly change and evolve—sometimes on a day to day basis. Current events change from day to day and so do hashtags.

New social networks continue to crop up allowing groups to engage with each other in new and novel ways (e.g. Periscope, Meerkat), and some social networks that were once considered to be established fade from the mainstream. This means that social media professionals need to be naturally interested—or better yet—fascinated by the social space, which would in turn make it easy for them to #ABL.

**What is an effective way for a brand to use a content calendar, but also be free to interact and be responsive in the moment?**

A content calendar gives a brand (and its executives!) a bird's-eye view of what they will be talking about, and thereby focusing on, for the coming month or year. It allows brands to orchestrate a strategic content narrative with ease, giving social media professionals more flexibility to create real-time content for trending topics relevant to their industry, respond to questions as they arise, and engage in community conversations.

**How can a brand effectively monitor and engage with social conversations taking place outside of the brand's official profile without appearing intrusive?**

It's important to understand the social norms of the platform you're engaging on. If it's Twitter, it's widely accepted that the conversation taking place is public. If the brand is polite (or funny!) and contributes something of value to the conversation, there shouldn't be a problem. If it's on social networks that are generally more private, for instance if the conversation is on a personal Facebook profile with public settings, it might be wise to hold off engagement unless that person specifically tagged your brand in the post.

**What tips would you suggest for brands to keep in mind when engaging in real-time in order to be authentic and interactive, but still on message with social media goals?**

Take some time upfront to develop a few key messages about your brand. Keep them in mind when interacting with your audience. A key message is what you want the public to know about your business and, ideally, should align with your social media goals. How you talk to your audience and what you emphasize about your business will flow from that central descriptor.

**In what ways, if any, does the information gathered from a social media campaign drive future strategy or engagement?**

*Kirsten connected us with Andy Au, Hootsuite's Social Content Lead, for his insights into this question.*

One of the things that make social media campaigns so exciting is the real-time feedback you receive. This can come qualitatively in the form of Twitter replies or Facebook comments but it also appears quantitatively—for example, URL clicks or video views.

For content marketing purposes, how well your content performs on social media is an early indicator of how well it will perform in general. We use our Twitter account to test certain topics to gauge our audience's appetite for it. Once we know something is a hit, we'll invest more resources to writing about it.

The information gathered early on in a campaign will affect our tactics for the remainder of the campaign. For example, we might prepare four to five separate blog posts that support a product release. Once we know which posts are resonating the most on social, we'll increase the frequency of social posts to the top-performing content and decrease the frequency to low-performing posts.

Similarly, our paid social ads are heavily influenced by our organic social performance. If a particular piece of content is working well organically, we will look to promote it using paid social ads—omitting any underperforming content.

*Kirsten Bailey is the Director of Online Education Products and New Product Growth at Hootsuite Media Inc.*

## Social Media and Crises

A crisis, by its very nature, is substantial. It is an event, or the perception of an event, that damages the relationships between a brand and the public, resulting in the reduction or inability of the organization to continue to fulfill its mission. Freberg and Palenchar (2012) explain that "crises come in various form and can impact an organization or individual at any time. In other words, crises are significant, disruptive events that often feature rapid onset" (p. 84). Reynolds and Seeger (2005) point out that communication during a crisis should "explain the specific event, identify likely consequences and outcomes, and provide specific harm-reducing information to affected communities in an honest, candid, prompt, accurate and complete manner" (p. 46). Ideally, organizations are able to identify potential crises before they occur. But, as already explained, there are many times when a crisis will strike without warning and with no prior chances to diffuse it.

Social media comes into play as part of the communication dissemination efforts during a crisis. The efforts to reply and provide accurate information during a crisis must be done in alignment with the organization's overall crisis plan. The integration with the organization's crisis response plan was explained in the social listening phase of campaign development. Due to the nature of high uncertainty during a crisis, it is important to provide needed information as quickly as possible to impacted audiences (Seeger, Sellnow, & Ulmer, 1998). This communication is done by specifically crafting messages for the stakeholders who have been identified as being affected, and developing messages to get accurate and helpful information to key audiences (Heath, Lee, & Ni, 2009).

While there are many categories of crises that an organization may face, in the context of the social media team it can be helpful to think in two large genres. crises that result due to something outside of social media; and crises that result due to activity or interaction via social media. It is important to explore not only how organizations can integrate social media effectively as a general part of their crises plans, but also how social media teams may best respond in the monitoring step of a social media campaign should a crises emerge due to social media.

### Crises External from Social Media

As defined above, crises can come about at any time and have dire consequences. Freberg and Palenchar (2012) point out that a crisis can be both an event that has occurred as well as a *perception* of events. Pearson and Clair (1998) explain the idea of crisis further by describing it as a "low-probability, high-impact event" (p. 60). Crises, then, can be events actually occurring or rumors of things that may happen. Because a crisis impacts the organization and stakeholders, rumors can sometimes be just as damaging as events that have occurred. Elements that contribute to crises include the magnitude of the crises, the control over the event, the reactions of the public to the event, and the potential that the event (if perceived as a crisis) will be one that will actually happen (Freberg & Palenchar, 2012). Because of the variety of forms a crisis can take, including workplace rumors, natural disasters, human errors, accidents, and many others, it is helpful to categorize crises in order for communicators to effectively engage with audiences in meaningful ways (Freberg & Palenchar, 2012, p. 84).

When an organization faces a crisis, utilizing social media to reach key audiences is helpful because it allows people to feel that they have more control over the crisis as well as feeling like they are connected into a community (Freberg & Palenchar, 2012). The information that is posted by the organization, however, needs to be in line with the overall messaging from the crisis response team. Most crisis plans for organizations include sections on specific types of crises that may hit an organization—be it a product recall, natural disaster, violence, or some other potentially disturbing event. As part of the crisis plan, it is helpful to pre-craft how social media can be used during the event to provide timely, authentic, transparent, and relevant information to the social media community. If there is a product recall, for example, sample posts could be created that include general language for how to return products and what steps consumers should take. In preparation for a natural disaster, drafting information that includes where to go for a shelter or tips on personal safety after an earthquake may be appropriate. It could also be that the organization will already have websites created with some basic information that will be "black" (not available) unless a crisis happens. If that is the case, it is also possible to pre-make posts that reference the site with the link so posts can go live immediately after a crisis hits. The goal is to have the social media strategy work in unison with other communication efforts, supporting the messaging strategies and responses of the crisis team.

### Crises Caused Within Social Media

The second genre of crises that a social media team should prepare for are those that originate within or due to social media. What exactly counts as a crisis in social media? It can be defined as: "a crisis issue that arises in or is amplified by social media, and results in negative mainstream media coverage, a change in business process, or financial loss" (Owyang, Jones, Tran, & Nguyen, 2011, p. 17). These kinds of crises regularly make the news. An example of this is when a BBC reporter mistakenly reported that Queen Elizabeth II had died, a tweet that, despite being deleted quickly, was already picked up by other news sources such as CNN and other publications (Elgot & Plunkett, 2015). Another example comes from KitchenAid, whose employee accidently sent an offensive tweet to President Obama about his dead grandmother. The brand quickly responded, apologizing and stating that the "tasteless joke in no way represents our values at KitchenAid, and that person won't be tweeting for us anymore" (Agnes, 2012). Still another social media case-study can be found in Papa John's response to a ten-word tweet from a customer that included a picture of the receipt from her recent order, which referred to the customer using a racial slur: "lady chinky eyes" (Duke, 2012). These kinds of crises go straight to the center of the driving force behind a brand: the perceived credibility and trustworthiness of the organization by the public. Timothy Coombs (2014), a leading crisis communication researcher, explained that social media crises are often reputational in nature. "Reputational concerns are important because an organizational reputation is a valued asset that must be cultivated and protected" (p. 23).

In order to effectively respond to a social media crises, there are three sources that may help determine the kind and nature of response required by the social media team (Coombs, 2014). Coombs suggests the three sources of social media crises are: 1) organizational misuses of social media, 2) dissatisfied customers, and 3) challenges in social media (p. 23).

The first type of crisis, and possibly the most common type to make headlines, is organizational misuse of social media. This type of social media crisis can be defined as when an "organization violates the norms of behavior in a particular social media channel" (Coombs, 2014, p. 23). Crises such as these can often be prevented with additional training of employees, research by organizations before creating content for social

*Figure 5.4* Contributors to Crises in Social Media

media, and a clear structure for addressing social media crises through identified roles, responsibilities, and approval processes (Owyang et al., 2011). A strong example of a crisis caused by organizational misuse of social media is when Digiorno decided to use the hashtag #WhyIStayed. The hashtag was a trending conversation that was a response to Ray Rice, an NFL player, being suspended after beating his wife. Women flocked to social media and used the hashtag #WhyIStayed to share their stories of what kept them in abusive and violent relationships. Without doing research or understanding the community having a conversation around that hashtag, Digiorno used the hashtag and added three simple words: "#WhyIStayed you had pizza." While this was a substantial debacle, largely criticized across social media platforms, Digiorno's social media team did take swift action to actively engage with the crisis. After rapidly deleting the tweet and apologizing for its offensive nature, the brand began to individually apologize to each and every user who had engaged with them regarding the inappropriate brand tweet. Rather than cutting and pasting in automated apologies, each tweet was customized and showed a high level of remorse, authenticity, and transparency. This incident, while a prime illustration of why brands should research before joining conversations, also shows a great example of an appropriate social response to individualized engagement through social media platforms (Sands, 2014).

The second source for crises within social media is customer dissatisfaction. Coombs (2014) explains that "Dissatisfied customer social media crises are really a customer relations problem rather than a crisis" (p. 23). However, social media is often used as a key part of public relations and, specifically, consumer or customer relations as it has the ability to foster two-way dialogue to resolve concerns. Key audiences have a higher likelihood of believing that an organization is trustworthy when there is two-way communication taking place (Freberg & Palenchar, 2012). In light of this, social media often becomes a primary platform for dealing with dissatisfied customers. In the airline industry, this type of crisis has a great deal of opportunity to happen. JetBlue is a leading example of a brand that uses social media to engage with customers and help resolve issues, minimizing crises due to dissatisfied customers. In 2010, JetBlue dedicated an entire team of people, 17 at the time, solely to interacting with customers on social media. At the time, they were one of the first airlines to make such a move (Piazza, 2014). Laurie Meacham, Manager of Customer Commitment and Social Media for JetBlue Airways, explained that for brands to be relevant and truly engage customer needs on social media, the content has to be authentic and relational. The humanization is essential for organizational success:

> There is a lot of vanity engagement happening out there. People talking about nothing and responding about nothing. We always

recognize that as a brand, we are a guest in this community. Brands came in uninvited. We need to earn the right to be here.
(quoted in Piazza, 2014, "Speaking in One Voice," para. 8)

Jet Blue has helped customers in sticky situations, like one customer who tweeted about not knowing why there was a $50 charge to be on standby for an earlier flight home. JetBlue was able to tweet back and address the customer's concerns without it becoming a significant issue (Kolowich, 2014). Another engagement was in response to a woman who was stuck in line so long at the airport she missed her flight. The social media representative responded to the woman via social media with tips to help make the flight in time, and also reached out to the gate to see if the woman would still be able to make her flight. Despite still missing the flight, the direct engagement and support from JetBlue led to a positive interaction rather than a negative response (Piazza, 2014, para. 4–6).

Sometimes, however, nothing will change the situation for key publics—in the case of JetBlue, flights will still be delayed or missed and fees may still be incurred. When customers are upset on social media and the brand's social media team cannot meaningfully engage or assist in the moment, it may be wise to wait to interact until there is more information or resources become available. Meacham refers to this type of situation as a DNE: Do Not Engage. "DNE is totally different from ignoring. We are taking note, and we will follow up where appropriate," she said (quoted in Piazza, 2014, "Speaking in One Voice," para. 16). The goal is not to ignore the customer or relationship, but to wait for the appropriate time to interact or directly contact them in a way that allows for follow-up that genuinely builds the relationship rather than simply creating more social noise. It is worth noting that the records of these types of interaction, whether one that had a positive outcome or one that resulted in a DNE, are important for long-term planning on social media and with crisis response.

The final genre of social media crises that begin within social media are called *challenges*, which is when key audiences believe an organization or brand has policies or behaviors that are inappropriate (Coombs, 2014, p. 23). "The core of the challenge is that stakeholders argue that the organization is acting irresponsibly. Those charges can erode reputations" (Coombs, 2014, p. 23). There are three types of challenges that may come up within a social media crisis. The first is *organic* and occurs when the expectations of the online brand community are not met by the organization's behaviors. This often happens when a brand fails to maintain a strong pulse on their online tribe's values, opinions, beliefs, and behaviors.

If organizational behaviors do not change to mirror those of the stakeholders, stakeholders will perceive the organization as violating their expectations. The misalignment of expectations can be a natural process because organizations often lag behind stakeholder expectations (value and belief changes).

(Coombs, 2014, p. 25)

A second type of challenge is an *exposé*, which arises "when stakeholders prove an organization's words are inconsistent with its actions" (Coombs, 2014, p. 25). This may happen when organizations claim to be environmentally friendly, but then information surfaces that show they are actually causing harm to the environment. Another example could be organizations that advocate for social justice but then are found to be using sweatshops to produce their products. Finally, the third kind of challenge is called a *villain* challenge, which, as the name suggests, is when groups claim that the organization itself is bad and needs to change. An excellent example of a challenge crisis can be found in the social media campaign launched by SeaWorld as part of their response to the documentary *BlackFish*, which accused SeaWorld of mistreating the animals, especially orca whales, within their facilities. Due to the boycotts and the effect on their bottom line as a result of the documentary, SeaWorld created a multi-million dollar campaign to repair its image by addressing public concerns and correcting misinformation presented in the film (Coffee, 2015). With over a million people contacting SeaWorld through PETA's online website, the brand was looking for a way to directly engage with their key audiences. The social media element to the campaign was a Q&A session with the hashtag #AskSeaWorld (Grisham, 2015). Unfortunately, the campaign was critically received. Rather than the kinds of questions the brand may have been hoping for, they received questions from critics involving why SeaWorld would breed more animals in captivity when it is already over-crowded and criticizing the animal care and death rates of SeaWorld orcas (Baker, 2015). These kinds of responses represented villain challenges, as they were directed at the very core of the brand, claiming that the organization itself was unethical.

Organizations can respond in a number of ways to challenge crises, resulting in the potential to maintain trust and credibility in the eyes of the public. It is very important to consult the public relations crises plan and guide in determining proper responses to crises situations, particularly if the nature of the crisis is a challenge, since it deals with the core reputation of the organization as a whole. Some ways professionals may decide to respond to challenges include: 1) refuting the claims made in the challenge, 2) reforming the behaviors or actions of the organization to align with the key audience expectations, and 3) repenting by acknowledging the fault and harm done and explaining what will be done to rectify the situation (Coombs, 2014, pp. 25–26). Responding to a challenge in social media is the most complex of all the social crises with which a team may deal. Be sure to "carefully assess the nature of the challenge before selecting a response strategy. Organic, exposé, and villain challenges have unique features that make different response strategies more or less effective" (Coombs, 2014, p. 26.)

## Social Fatigue

One final area to address within the monitoring step of a social media campaign, though an area that often receives very little focus, deals with social media fatigue. *Social fatigue* is when the level of interaction and repetitive nature of social media causes individuals to shut-down or tune-out. There are two dimensions that brands should consider: fatigue with their key publics, and fatigue within the organization's own social media channels.

### Fatigue among Key Publics

In 2012, Google released a study titled "The New Multi-screen World: Understanding Cross-Platform Consumer Behavior." Their findings reveal a lot about what key stakeholders experience on a daily basis and why social media fatigue seems to be a growing phenomenon in society. For example, while it was already stated that there are more devices connected to the Internet than there are people in the world (Bennett, 2013), Google (2012) also found that 90% of all media interaction is "screen-based" or through technology platforms like television, phones, and computers (Slide 8). With the majority of media interaction taking place via screens, it is also helpful to understand two main ways people choose to consume information when faced with using a phone or a tablet or a laptop or some other device. The first way people consume information is called *sequential usage*, and is when people move "from one device to another at different times to accomplish a task" (Slide 17). The other type of consumption is *simultaneous usage*, which is when people use "more than one device at the same time for either a related or unrelated activity" (Slide 17). Out of the two ways to consume information, sequential usage is the most common, with 90% of people preferring that method of consumption. For those that do choose to use the simultaneous approach to media consumption, smartphones are the most frequent companion to other media, such as a laptop, TV, or tablet (Slide 25). While some people use multiple screens to finish a given task, many (78%) are simply multi-tasking while using multiple devices (Slide 27). In short, people are highly connected across multiple media, consistently engaging in activities that fragment attention and pull for focus.

When users engage with a brand on social media, it is simply one more interaction (whether sequentially placed in the middle of other activity or simultaneously while they are completing other tasks within their day). This has led to what Michael Brito (2014) calls "CADD" or Customer Attention Deficit Disorder. With the millions of status updates, tweets, and videos that pour into the social world every hour, combined with the constant pull for attention between devices and within everyday life activities, organizations must find relevant connections to truly engage people. "We're inundated daily with content and media that we just don't care about, and it's the sole reason why we create relevance filters," Brito suggests (p. 20). Relevance filters are the strata that individuals use to identify information to sort, prioritize, and relegate within the digital world. To combat being tuned out and blocked by key publics' relevance filters, it is important to remember what social media is all about: relationships. Ted Coiné and Mark Babbitt (2014) frame this by being about "More social. Less media" when they say:

> We recognize that a deeply personal relationship and genuine influence occur far more often when you hear the other people's voices, when you see their body language, when you look into their eyes. After all, 140 characters offer little insight into another person's soul. Pick up the phone. Arrange a Skype call. Buy a cup of coffee.
>
> (p. 221)

Social media campaign engagement requires a strong commitment to the humanization of communication, not mechanization. Social media is one connection point for brands and organizations with people—not the *only* connection. Actively find ways to integrate social media into other types of engagement. Perhaps this will mean getting a Twitter user's phone number and passing that on to customer service. It may involve inviting a social media community to a real-time event, to meet and connect with people. Whatever seems to be the best fit for the brand, remember that social media is about people. Use social to build authentic relationships that thrive in the digital and face-to-face world.

### Organizational Social Media Fatigue

Organizations can also experience fatigue in social media. This can stem from having too many platforms and not enough resources to effectively engage or from lacking a clear vision for why social media supports the brand's vision. Just like individuals, brands should carefully consider the capacity to maintain authentic relationships within social media. Rebecca Lieb (2012) points out the challenge to engage strategically on social media:

> Like consumers, brands are challenged to make social channel choices. Spreading themselves too thin in an effort to be everywhere, for everyone, leads to challenges few brands are prepared to meet. The demands of continual parallel content creation. The ability to react and respond to earned media in multiple social channels.
>
> ("When to Invest Time in the New New Thing?" para. 5)

Essentially, brands must use discretion to avoid social media burn-out. Ted Coiné and Mark Babbitt (2014) give three key ways brands can avoid feeding in to social media fatigue. First, be conscious that the organization is not contributing negative content, or simply creating more social noise in an already over-saturated media environment. Make each post, tweet, and snap meaningful, having been designed with a purpose. Second, "deliberately be a relentless giver" in social media by highlighting others, being a resource, and genuinely interacting with people (p. 221). Finally, avoid being a "social echo chamber" (p. 221). In other words, if the brand is simply reposting what already was posted again and again and is no longer contributing original content to the social media community, take some time away. Give the brand space to be silent if there is nothing significant to contribute into the social world.

For brands on social media to be relevant, breaking through the relevance filters of users, they must stay authentically engaged. Content simply cannot be regurgitated because nothing new is available. Adding to noise in social media does not help an organization stand apart or build stronger relationships. Rather, refocus on the purpose of social media, the ways for the brand to enhance relationships, and then develop interaction based on those elements.

## KEY CONCEPT SNAPSHOT

1. Content calendars provide a way to harmonize communication on behalf of brands, developing a tapestry of unified interaction for the vision of the organization's values.
2. Crises on social media are going to happen—brands that are truly strategic in social media prepare for them *before* they occur, allowing a proactive approach to social media during crises rather than reactive.
3. Social media is all about *relationships*. Monitoring and responding to people in social spaces shows authenticity and builds trust.
4. Relevance filters require brands to focus on creating meaningful and relevant content in social media in order to avoid social fatigue within their brand community.

## Suggested Reading

Deen, H., & Hendricks, J. (2013). *Social media and strategic communications*. Houndmills, Basingstoke, Hampshire: Palgrave Macmillan.

Hyatt, M. (2012). *Platform: Get noticed in a noisy world*. Nashville, TN: Thomas Nelson.

Kerns, C. (2014). *Trendology: Building an advantage through data-driven real-time marketing*. New York: Palgrave Macmillan.

## References

*Note*: All website URLs accessed February 4, 2016.

Agnes, M. (2012, Oct. 4). KitchenAid: An excellent example of successful crisis management. *MelissaAgnes.com*. Retrieved from: http://melissaagnes.com/kitchenaid-an-excellent-example-in-social-media-crisis-communications/

Baer, J. (n.d.). 42 percent of consumers complaining in social media expect 60 minute response time. *Convince & Convert*. Retrieved from: www.convinceandconvert.com/social-media-research/42-percent-of-consumers-complaining-in-social-media-expect-60-minute-response-time/

Baker, D. (2015, March 27). "Ask SeaWorld" Twitter campaign chum in the water for critics. *The San Diego Union Tribune*. Retrieved from: www.utsandiego.com/news/2015/mar/27/ask-seaworld-twitter-campaign/

Bennett, S. (2013, Jan. 4). 100 amazing social media statistics, facts and figures [Infographic]. *Adweek*. Retrieved from: www.adweek.com/socialtimes/100-social-media-stats/475180

Brito, M. (2014). *Your brand, the next media company: How a social business strategy enables better content, smarter marketing, and deeper customer relationships*. Indianapolis, IN: Que.

Coffee, P. (2015, March 24). SeaWorld launched multi-million dollar reputation campaign. *PRNewser*. Retrieved from: www.adweek.com/prnewser/seaworld-launches-multi-million-dollar-reputation-campaign/111366

Coiné, T., & Babbitt, M. (2014). *A world gone social: How companies must adapt to survive*. New York: AMACOM, American Management Association.

Coombs, W. T. (2014). *Ongoing crisis communication: Planning, managing, and responding*. Thousand Oaks, CA: SAGE.

Duke, A. (2012, Jan. 8). Papa John's apologizes for receipt's racial slur. *CNN*. Retrieved from: www.cnn.com/2012/01/08/us/new-york-papa-johns-receipt/

Elgot, J., & Plunkett, J. (2015, June 3). Rogue BBC tweet sparks global news alert about Queen's health. *The Guardian*. Retrieved from: www.theguardian.com/uk-news/2015/jun/03/queens-health-bbc-tweet-global-news-alert

Freberg, K., & Palenchar, M. (2012). Convergence of digital negotiation and risk challenges: Strategic implications of social media for risk and crisis communication. In A. Handley, & C. C. Chapman (Eds.) *Content rules: How to create killer blogs, podcasts, videos, ebooks, webinars (and more) that engage customers and ignite your business* (pp. 83–100). Hoboken, NJ: Wiley.

Google. (2012, Aug.). The new multi-screen world: Understanding cross-platform consumer behavior. *Google*. Retrieved from: https://think.withgoogle.com/databoard/media/pdfs/the-new-multi-screen-world-study_research-studies.pdf

Grisham, L. (2015, March 25). "Ask SeaWorld" ad campaign draws criticism. *USA Today*. Retrieved from: www.usatoday.com/story/news/nation-now/2015/03/25/seaworld-killer-whales-ad-campaign/70422606/

Handley, A., & Chapman, C. C. (2012). *Content rules: How to create killer blogs, podcasts, videos, ebooks, webinars (and more) that engage customers and ignite your business*. Hoboken, NJ: Wiley.

Heath, R. L., Lee, J., & Ni, L. (2009). Crisis and risk approaches to emergency management planning and communication: The role of similarity and sensitivity. *Journal of Public Relations Research*, 21(2), 123–141.

Kerns, C. (2014). *Trendology: Building an advantage through data-driven real-time marketing*. New York: Palgrave Macmillan.

Kolowich, L. (2014, July 28). Delighting people in 140 characters: An inside look at JetBlue's customer service success. *Hub Spot*. Retrieved from: http://blog.hubspot.com/marketing/jetblue-customer-service-twitter

Lieb, R. (2012, March 19). How real is social media fatigue? *Marketing Land*. Retrieved from: http://marketingland.com/how-real-is-social-media-fatigue-7665

Owyang, J., Jones, A., Tran, C., & Nguyen, A. (2011, Aug. 31). Social business readiness: How advanced companies prepare internally. *Altimeter*. Retrieved from: www.slideshare.net/jeremiah_owyang/social-readiness-how-advanced-companies-prepare

Pearson, C. M., & Clair, J. A. (1998). Reframing crisis management. *The Academy of Management Review,* 23(1), 59–76.

Piazza, J. (2014, July 29). "The secret of JetBlue's media success? Stay at home moms, cat memes – and a sense of humor. *Yahoo Travel*. Retrieved from: https://www.yahoo.com/travel/the-secrets-of-jetblues-social-media-success-93024204957.html

Reynolds, B., & Seeger, M.W. (2005). Crisis and emergency risk communication as an integrative model. *Journal of Health Communication,* 10, 43–55.

Sands, K. (2014, Sept. 9). A lesson in crisis communications, courtesy of DiGiorno. *Huffington Post*. Retrieved from: www.huffingtonpost.com/katrina-sands/a-lesson-in-crisis-commun_b_5794122.html

Schaefer, M. (2012). *Return on influence: The revolutionary power of Klout, social scoring, and influence marketing.* New York: McGraw-Hill.

Seeger, M. W., Sellnow, T. L., & Ulmer, R. R. (1998). Communication, organization and crisis. In M. E. Roloff (Ed.), *Communication Yearbook 21.* Thousand Oaks, CA: SAGE.

Wilcox, D., & Cameron, G. (2009). *Public relations: Strategies and tactics.* Boston: Pearson/Allyn and Bacon.

# Chapter 6

# Step 4: Evaluation

## Showcasing Success and Growth Opportunities

> Social media experts should champion robust evaluation of each campaign as it not only provides evidence and support for the value of social media within a brand's overall communication efforts, but also because evaluation has a heuristic element that allows for future growth and greater expertise within the social world.

The final step in developing and managing social media campaigns is evaluating the effectiveness of the efforts. This step is critical in providing accountability and illustrating the value of social media within an organization. It is important, before developing the framework for evaluation, to understand the difference between *measurement* and *counting*. People often, unfortunately, oversimplify social media evaluation by viewing it as a simple set of numbers to be counted or gathered. The truth of the matter is that social media evaluation and measurement is much more rigorous than this. It requires social media professionals to *apply* their expertise into the measurements that are gathered and to then develop meaningful applications from the data. Katie Delahaye Paine (2011) explains it this way:

> *Counting* just adds things up and gets a total. *Measurement* takes those totals, analyzes what they mean, and uses that meaning to improve business practices. Measurement of your process and results—where you spend your time and money and what you get out of it—provides data necessary to make sound decisions. It helps you set priorities, allocate resources, and make choices. Without it, hunches and gut feelings prevail. Without it, mistakes get made and no one learns from them.
>
> (p. 5)

There are a variety of metrics that are useful in the evaluation step for campaigns. To lay the foundation for understanding evaluation, it is helpful to reflect on the way data is used throughout a social media campaign. After reviewing the use of data throughout the life-cycle of a campaign, the three levels to campaign evaluation will be explained: preparation, implementation, and impact. Within each of these levels, specific processes and metrics that are important will be discussed.

## Data Use Throughout a Social Media Campaign

Social media efforts should be driven by real-time activities: what audiences are doing, responding to, talking about, and engaging with all play a crucial role in social strategy. Data is gathered throughout a campaign to inform both decisions and strategies for brands. Sometimes the data gathered is on base metrics such as the number of likes, followers, comments, or mentions. However, as was discussed earlier, there are other kinds of metrics that are also helpful; these include identifying influencers, measuring tone, and monitoring conversions. While this chapter focuses on data collection, analysis, and interpretation within Step 4 (Evaluation), recognizing how a brand uses data throughout the entire campaign is an important competency.

### Social Listening

During the first step of the campaign, social media strategists gather formative data on: the organization, current social media platforms, brand communities, and competition. This social listening phase informs the entire design of the campaign in Step 2, Strategic Design.

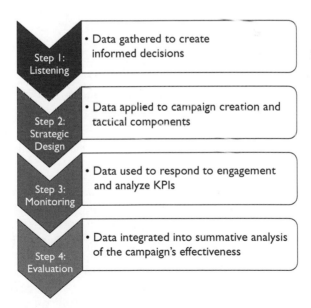

- Data gathered to create informed decisions

Step 1: Listening

- Data applied to campaign creation and tactical components

Step 2: Strategic Design

- Data used to respond to engagement and analyze KPIs

Step 3: Monitoring

- Data integrated into summative analysis of the campaign's effectiveness

Step 4: Evaluation

*Figure 6.1* Data Use Throughout a Campaign

### Strategic Design

The formative research gathered in Step 1 allows for social media professionals to craft engaging and dynamic campaigns, centered around SMART, outcome-based objectives. The entire strategic design phase is data-informed and data-driven in its creation.

### Implementation and Monitoring

In the third step, Implementation, strategists put into action the program that was created and designed for social media. In addition, data plays a crucial role in this step because it drives informed engagement. In the world of social media, interaction with the publics should never be dissected from monitoring. As a brand monitors the campaign, measuring reach, engagement, and impact of social media interaction, a wealth of information is gleaned. First, the brand understands what is working within the campaign. Second, the brand will also be alerted when the brand community interacts, in what way the community is interacting, and the tone or intent of the interaction. This information informs how the brand should respond, who needs to be included in the response, and ultimately helps define what type of communication the brand community is expecting from the organization. This kind of data monitoring during a campaign ensures that the social media campaign is achieving its intended purpose.

### Evaluation

Finally, at the close of a campaign, social media professionals gather *summative* data. This information is used not only to evaluate whether a campaign was successful but also to lay a foundation for the listening phase of future campaigns. Step 4 collects and interprets data in order to summarize what the campaign achieved.

The ability to gather information, which informs and helps develop business intelligence, through social media has revolutionized the ways organizations can apply meaningful data to strategic decisions and future activity. Oliver Blanchard (2011) identifies this powerful ability as the combination of velocity and specificity:

> The velocity with which organizations can collect specific data, gather business intelligence, and measure the impact of a particular activity at any given time by using social media is astounding. Two rarely discussed key benefits to emerge from the marriage of social media and business measurement are velocity and specificity. Velocity is important to the success of a social media program because the speed with which intelligence reaches a decision maker will impact the speed with which he can respond to a market opportunity.
>
> ("Building Velocity and Specificity," para. 4–5)

In other words, the ability to quickly gather data, have that information reach key strategists, and take action as a result of the specific detail empowers organizations to effectively engage with key stakeholders like never before in organizational history.

While data is used throughout a campaign, the evaluation portion is particularly rich in measurement gathering and interpretation. Determining the effectiveness of a campaign is no small task—which is why it is valuable to understand the many elements that should be evaluated within a campaign.

## Components to Evaluation

Expert evaluation requires social media professionals to analyze every element of a campaign—from start to finish. In order to accomplish this, there are three main sections that should each be investigated in order to determine the total effectiveness of a campaign. These sections are: Preparation, Implementation, and Impact (Broom & Sha, 2013).

- *Preparation* evaluates items from the listening and strategic design stages of the campaign. The goal is to assess whether, prior to launching the social media campaign, proper information was in place and whether the strategic design was correctly developed from the data.
- *Implementation* evaluates the third stage of the social media campaign, examining whether information was delivered at the correct time, whether it reached the identified audiences, and the nature of the engagement that occurred as a result of the engagement.
- *Impact* relates to the specific objectives that were established for the campaign in order to achieve the overall goal of the campaign.

What may already be apparent is the fact that every social media campaign evaluation has a plethora of data to mine through in order to provide an effective analysis. It is important to assess what is most critical

| Evaluation | | |
|---|---|---|
| **Preparation** | **Implementation** | **Impact** |
| • Formative Research Review | • Social Media Dashboard KPIs | • SMART, Outcome-based Objectives |
| • Strategic Design Analysis | • Message Reach | • Consumption Metrics |
| • Presentation | • Engagement | • Sharing Metrics |
| | | • Actionable Metrics |

*Figure 6.2* Elements to Evaluation

for the brand to understand from the campaign in order to evaluate not only the campaign's impact, but to strategically move forward in future social media campaigns. That is why, within each of these areas, each brand will need to evaluate data based on their individual needs and values.

While some may argue that, essentially, the evaluation stage is solely to measure the impact, or return on investment (ROI), of a social media campaign and the ultimate contribution to the organization, this perspective fails to recognize the value that can be gained by an in-depth exploration of the entire campaign. In order to understand the full value of social media it is helpful to have a more nuanced approach that allows social media strategists to articulate the multiple ways social media advances the organizational goals and objectives.

## Preparation

Evaluation of a social media campaign's preparation involves identifying whether everything was in place that needed to be prior to launching the actual campaign. A strong foundation, or preparation, gives life to a strategic campaign. On the other hand, a weak or incomplete preparation of a social media campaign is often the root cause for failures. Jim Sterne (2010) points out the value of preparation by reminding strategists of the need for concrete planning before engaging in social media:

> Why are you even bothering with social media? If you don't know, you do not want to step in blindly. This is the realm of public opinion and customer conversations. You do not want to blunder onto the scene without a clear idea of why you are there and what you want out of it. Not only are you sure to make hash of it, anything you measure will be context free and worse than useless.
>
> (p. xxvii)

Within the evaluation of preparation in a campaign, three main areas to consider are: 1) the formative research that was gathered in listening, 2) the program's strategic design, and 3) the presentation content.

### Formative Research

Formative research, which helps form the foundation for campaigns, is important as it helps identify key elements that, if missing or incorrect, could result in a less effective campaign. It is important, therefore, to consider whether during the formative research correct information was available to identify all the primary objectives of the campaign, key audiences, keywords, organizational structural needs, and other elements that were important to the success of the campaign. For example, were all the keywords and phrases used by the SEO team that were provided to the social media team integrated into the messaging of the social media campaign? Did the market research provide the necessary information to effectively develop audience profiles for the social media brand community? Did the information available regarding other communication from the brand during the campaign thoroughly explain times that were effective (or ineffective) to communicate?

Next, identify whether any assumptions about or interpretations of the information were incorrect. For example, were the tones of the conversations in social media correctly identified, or was it later realized that some were much more positive (or negative) than originally thought? Perhaps it was assumed that certain social media users were influencers, only to later realize that they did not have a significant role within the social media platform the brand was using. Essentially, in this stage, each *application* of data that was made in order to determine strategy should be reviewed for accuracy and completeness.

Finally, there should be an evaluation of the documents that were available during the course of the social media campaign. It is important to identify, for the increased success of future campaigns, any documents that were needed but were not available. It could be something like the lack of a correct crisis response policy, which resulted in difficulties during the campaign. It could be that the web development team had no online user policies and the social media team ended up having less efficiency in meeting deadlines for campaign launches as a result. Whatever was not available, as well as the implication of not having these resources, should be noted. It is important to note that this final category is not a blame-placing section. It is simply an identifier of what could have delayed, inhibited, or influenced later results in the campaign.

*Strategic Design*

The next part to evaluating the preparation of the campaign is to review the strategic design. Begin by performing a top-down review of the campaign strategy:

- Was the goal appropriate for the organization's current need and purpose of social media?
- Were the audiences that were selected for each goal actually the ones that needed to be involved in ensuring the goal was met? Were there any that should have been removed or added?
- Was each objective SMART (strategic, measurable, achievable, relevant, and timely)? In addition, were the objectives outcome-based (reliant on an action that the online communities would take)?
- Did each strategy specifically relate to the direct success of the objective it was supporting? Were any of the strategies less effective or,

potentially, would have been more effective if they had been used somewhere else in the campaign?

- Were all tactics identified correctly? Should any have been added or removed?

Next, it is important to return to the social media strategic plan and identify whether the social media campaign goal(s) supported the overall mission of the organization. Identifying how every campaign that is launched supports the overall vision of social media within the brand is a key part to program evaluation. In addition, review the purpose statement for each social media platform and evaluate whether the strategies and tactics that were implemented during the campaign supported those purposes.

Finally, evaluate the brand's persona and tone throughout the campaign. To do this, review not only the posts from the content calendar, but also the engagement responses that were sent by the brand throughout a campaign. Review each tweet, post, reply, comment, and mention to determine if the organization's social voice was consistent with the brand's persona, tone, and purpose of the campaign. In addition to noting effective posts and content that was particularly relevant to the community, also identify anything that was not consistent and review what was missing or should have been added.

### Presentation

The last component to evaluating the preparation for the social media campaign is to look at the creative pieces that were designed and the overall presentation of the brand throughout the campaign. Begin by reviewing the social profiles the brand used. Provide feedback on the quality of the profile's presentation including images used, the positioning of any information (such as in the "About" section), the connected nature of the social channel to other properties of the brand (such as links to the website or other social media platforms), and the general impression of the brand that was given by each platform. Was it clear that the platform was the official presence of the brand on that social media channel? Was there any indication that highlighted the current campaign on the profile, while keeping the general look and feel of the brand? Note any inconsistencies, strengths, or points of feedback.

Next, assess the quality of the creative content used throughout the campaign. The goal is that the quality of content provided in videos, photos, infographics, memes, etc. would match the brand's persona and tone appropriately, while effectively delivering the intended campaign messages. Be sure to note any creative content pieces that were particularly strong and highly reflective of the brand, as well as those which were weak and did not stay true to the brand persona. In addition, comment on any pieces that seemed to effectively portray the campaign message as well as those, if any, that were less suited to the purpose. For example, it might be noted that while a vine was professionally created and high quality, it was less effective at delivering a message for the campaign. Or, perhaps an image that was designed carried a strong message but was pixelated. It is important to recognize that the evaluation is not only to identify opportunities for future growth but also strengths. Make sure to identify specific elements of a campaign that were excellent in presentation quality. These can serve as models for future campaigns and initiatives.

## Implementation

After evaluating the preparation that was involved for a campaign to launch, it is helpful to evaluate the effectiveness of the actual implementation and engagement of the campaign. In this portion, the content calendar monitoring section will come in especially handy. The purpose of evaluating the implementation section is not only to analyze the actual flow of communication, but also to review key progress indicators (KPIs). As a reminder, a KPI is a number that represents progress toward a given goal by an organization. They are the areas that are measured to illustrate whether, throughout a campaign, an objective is being achieved or if the efforts are falling short. Eric Peterson (2006) explains this by saying, "Key performance indicators are designed to summarize meaningfully compared data" (Slide 8). The purpose of KPIs is to allow large data to be explained in a simple, concise manner throughout the course of a campaign. Peterson suggests that KPIs are "a response to a general organizational fear of big, ugly spreadsheets and complex applications. The big idea behind KPIs is that you're taking technical data and presenting it using business-relevant language" (Slide 7). To begin analyzing KPIs, each social media platform has a dashboard of information to review.

### Social Media Dashboard Analytics

Before truly being able to make meaning of the data in a unified manner for evaluation, it is helpful to understand the kind of information that can be gathered from each platform's analytics, which might serve as KPIs. Essentially, brands should identify *who* is doing *what* with *which* kinds of content, *when* it is happening, and *how* that supports the vision of the brand being on social media. That is the purpose of metrics.

Social media platforms have internal analytic options to help brands understand the effectiveness of their content and how the brand communities are interacting. While the social media analytics within each platform differ in terminology and setup, social media professionals who understand the basic intent of analytic measurements can successfully interpret information from each platform. For example, on Instagram, followers can like or comment on a photo, and that is valuable for a brand to know. But on YouTube, there are no likes—there are thumbs-up, which are comparable. But beyond that, the more meaningful interaction would be to know whether people are watching videos and subscribing to the channel. Platform analytics, therefore, need to reflect the kind of engagement that is possible and meaningful on a given platform.

By understanding Facebook's Insights, one of the most robust and leading internal analytic social dashboards, many of the other metrics on social sites will make sense. There are also external social media evaluation methods that can be applied to help with evaluation, which will be explored later in the chapter.

## FACEBOOK

Facebook's analytics, which are called Insights, are available to any brand that has an official page within Facebook. Within Insights, there are seven main areas that can be used to gather data. Each of the tabs has a unique purpose and presentation of information regarding campaign initiatives.

*Overview*   The Overview tab is the first place that Insights will display and it serves as a one-stop review. This tab gives metrics such as page likes, post reach, and engagement for a seven-day period. It is also possible to do a review of the most recent posts and their performance. Finally, at

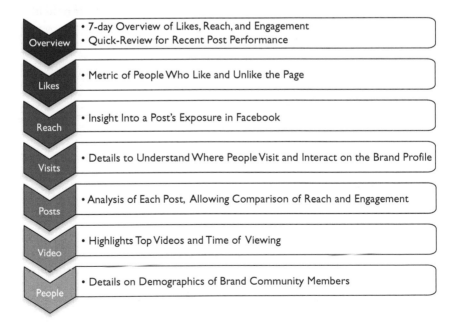

*Figure 6.3* Facebook Insight Data

the bottom of the overview tab there is a "Pages to Watch" measurement, which monitors key competition and shows the total likes, new page likes, number of posts for the week, and engagement for each brand competitor that was added to the list. This is a quick way to not only determine general activity for the week by the brand but also to provide a comparative analysis for competition. The information from this tab is a great overview of the recent activity, but it is important to drill down into the information further in order to really understand what is happening on the social platform.

*Likes* For every tab except the Overview, it is important to set the date-range that is to be analyzed. This will allow evaluation to span the entire campaign period, versus the week that shows in the Overview. The Likes tab is the place to go in order to understand general metrics for likes, unlikes, and paid likes throughout the life-cycle of a campaign. The goal is to allow brands to determine not only how many likes they have, but when they are receiving likes and from where they are coming.

Two key areas to look for in this tab include: 1) a chart that illustrates the growth (or decline) in page likes over the set time-period, providing a helpful visual to incorporate into brand evaluation reports; and 2) a chart that illustrates the number of net likes, which highlights the total new likes with the subtraction of unlikes for the page. This metric allows analysts to recognize the overall impact to the brand community as a result of a campaign initiative. In addition, this chart is also helpful because it will show additional information regarding each like, unlike, or paid like within the campaign.

**Meaningful Application:** Use data from the Likes tab to:

1. Compare the effectiveness of posts and strategies in social media by examining the dates which showed spikes in likes on the page, which helps in identifying content that was particularly meaningful to the brand community.
2. Determine whether there are certain content or post topics that resulted in people leaving the social community, indicating messaging to avoid in the future.
3. Review where likes initiated from within Facebook. For example, it is possible to compare whether likes are happening more often when people visit the official page, whether they simply click like after seeing a post in the News Feed, or whether it was a result of a page suggestion that was paid for by the brand.

Before moving on to the information available on the next tab, it is important to note that some brands fall into the trap of using metrics from this tab as the prime indicator of success in Facebook initiatives. It is important to review the SMART, outcome-based objectives for a campaign.

Likes often support reaching those objectives but usually are not the primary indicator that the campaign was successful.

Listing thousands of new likes can have shock value, seeming to indicate that a social media campaign was wildly successful, which may be why it is so often used when compiling reports on social media's impact. However, because this metric is so often overused as a claim to success, while often, in reality, it is not a *key* progress indicator for an objective of the campaign, it is sometimes called a *vanity* metric. Vanity metrics are those that look awesome and seem appealing, but, when examined further, do not necessarily have strong support for the purpose of the organization on social media. It is possible, for example, pages with thousands of likes actually result in very little engagement among the brand community. That is why it is important to consider all the metrics in *context* and provide meaningful evaluation based on the information.

*Reach*    The next tab is called Reach and will provide analysis regarding specific content and exposure within Facebook. There are five graphs to look at in the Reach tab.

1.  The first graph shows how many people were exposed to a post during a specific date. Keep in mind, a post will have more reach if people are commenting, liking, and sharing it, as it then shows in more News Feeds and has the potential to reach a much larger audience.
2.  On the Post Reach chart, a comparison of reach by organic versus paid posts is shown.
3.  The Likes, Comments, Shares chart displays activities that were happening in the brand community on given dates, which provides a connection to understand why certain posts had enhanced reach during given time-periods.
4.  The Hide, Report as Spam and Unlikes chart reveals whether content was negatively received by the brand community during certain time-periods. If a brand has data spikes in this chart, consider reviewing the content posted on those days to identify the type of content that caused this reaction in the social media community.
5.  The final chart in this section, Total Reach, calculates the number of people who are exposed to any activity from the entire page during a campaign, instead of just exposed as a result of a post. The Total Reach metric is then, understandably, typically higher than the Post Reach metrics, as it calculates all activity of a page during the campaign period specified.

**Meaningful Application:** Use data from the Reach tab to:

1.  Identify time-periods that were particularly influential during the campaign, illustrated by increased reach of either posts or the Total

Posts chart. Identify whether this relates to specific strategies being more influential within the campaign compared to other strategies.

2. Review the perception of content by the brand community, examining whether content was poorly received either by being hidden, reported as spam, or unliked. Make note of the kinds of data that create that response in the brand community.

*Visits*    Visits is the next tab and will illustrate the various portions of a Facebook page that were viewed by users over the course of the campaign. For example, it is possible to see how many people are visiting a timeline versus a tab that may have been created on a Facebook page for a promotion or giveaway. The first chart shows the number of times each section on a brand's page was viewed and the second chart shows external referrals to the brand's page.

**Meaningful Application:** Use data from the Visits tab to:

1. Analyze which areas of the page are most important to the brand community, indicated by a high number of visits. Are certain tactics or strategies tied to this success?
2. Consider whether a tab created for the campaign (potentially a contest tab or information tab) received visits. High numbers of visits could be an indicator that the tab was effective in engaging the brand community while low visits would seem to indicate that the tab did not fulfill its purpose throughout the campaign.
3. Analyze the external referral sites that are driving traffic to the page. Consider what is causing people to come from those sources and whether any were connected as a direct tactic within the campaign initiative.

*Posts*    Perhaps one of the most important tabs to review is the Posts tab. This will show data based on each content piece placed in Facebook. While this information is available in Reach, the presentation and analysis available in the Posts tab is quite powerful. The first area to consider in the Posts tab is a general overview of performance for posts. The section includes the "When Your Fans are Online" chart, which will show what dates and times the brand's audience is online. It is also possible to select "Post Types" to understand the type of posts on the page that have the highest reach and engagement, such as posts with links versus posts with photos. And finally, "Top Posts from Pages You Watch" will reveal which posts from the competition had the highest reach and engagement over the time period selected.

The second, and most robust part to this tab, is the Post Analytic section. All posts published throughout the life-cycle of the campaign will be listed in this table. The table can be sorted and analyzed according to a number of factors including: the date and time of publication, the classification of the post (link/photo), targeting of the post (the audience who could see the post), reach, and engagement. The table will provide the exact content of the post and the option to "boost" the post, which is paid promotion, which can be helpful for future paid strategies. The information in this table can be customized to display information on: 1) organic posts versus paid posts, 2) engagement and reach of posts by fans and non-fans, and 3) specific kinds of engagement, such as a like or share, or negative types of engagement (such as hides or spam reports). In early 2016, Facebook launched the option for reactions to posts, beyond just simply liking content. This means that users can hit the six following options for each post: like, love, haha, wow, sad, and angry. To see the complete breakdown of reactions to a post, as well as other analytic data, simply select an individual post and click it within the All Posts Published report.

**Meaningful Application:** Use data from the Posts tab to:

1.  Review the "When Your Fans are Online" chart and evaluate whether timing and delivery of messages was strong in a campaign. Take note of the specific times that posts were most effective and times when they were less effective.
2.  Review the post types to see which kinds of content had the greatest reach and engagement. Evaluate the engagement type to understand what type of behavior is likely to be triggered in the brand community (sharing, commenting, etc.) by certain kinds of posts. Did these behaviors align with the specified desired audience behavior identified on the content calendar created for the campaign?
3.  Analyze the posts' impact among both the brand community and "non-fans" or people outside of the brand community who were exposed to the posts through connections with members of the brand community. This can help determine which types of content are best suited to bring new members into a brand community.
4.  Review the "Top Posts from Pages You Watch" to understand the types of posts that seem most effective from the competition and compare that to the post information from the campaign. It may help to confirm that the message and strategic design was strong or that information should have been presented differently.

*Video*   A newer tab in Facebook's Insights, this tab has three charts: one to show videos that were watched for more than 3 seconds, one to show videos that were watched for more than 30 seconds, and one which shows the top videos for the page.

**Meaningful Application:** Use data from the Video tab to:

1.  Determine not only which kinds of videos are watched, but which are watched for longer periods. Video is the fastest growing type of engagement content in social media, and this report will indicate the kinds of video that are most influential in the brand community.

2. Identify the theme, style, and content of videos that resonate the most with the social media community to use in future campaigns and to evaluate whether the design of the videos for the social media campaign was effective.

*People*  This is the final tab and will provide base-level demographics of the brand community, people that are reached through the brand's content, and people engaged through the brand's content. It is possible to identify gender, age, country, city, and language demographics for each of those categories.

**Meaningful Application:** Use data from the People tab to:

1. Evaluate the profile of the audience the campaign was designed to reach and whether the platform engaged the key publics.
2. Determine whether the campaign engaged any new audiences that may not have been considered as a primary group within the campaign.

While other social sites may not have as much content in the analytics dashboard compared to Facebook, there is still a lot of valuable information. Many social media sites measure similar metrics, or key progress indicators, that can be evaluated by brands but may have different names for them. As previously stated, that is why it is important to understand the purpose of metrics in social media so that professionals can apply that concept to any type of metric or data available from a social platform. KPIs measure meaningful behaviors within a social media platform.

TWITTER

Twitter analytics have many similar metrics to Facebook. There are three main tabs to understand: Home, Tweets, and Followers.

*Home*  As with the main Overview tab in Facebook, the Twitter Home tab gives a snapshot of all that is happening, but instead of a week, it provides information on the last 28 days for a Twitter account. After identifying Tweets, Tweet Impressions (similar to Reach in Facebook), Profile Visits, Mentions, and Followers, the Home tab gives an overview of each month. The month sections include the top tweet, top follower, top mention, top media, and basic metrics such as tweets sent during the month, profile visits, new followers gained, tweet impressions, and mentions.

*Tweets*  As with the Home tab, the Tweets tab begins with a total number of impressions, the average number of impressions earned per day, and the engagement metric averages. Within this tab, there are four ways to view content from the month: 1) Tweets, which shows all posts, 2) Top Tweets, which highlights the most effective tweets, 3) Tweets and Replies, which shows not only the tweets from the brand, but each reply throughout the time period, and 4) Promoted, which are tweets that are paid for, in order to have higher prominence and impressions.

No matter what view the information is being analyzed through, the chart will show: 1) Impressions, which is how many people on Twitter saw the Tweet; 2) Engagement, which is a measurement of any kind of activity including clicking a link or hashtag, following, replying, or retweeting; and 3) Engagement Rate, which is a percentage calculated by dividing the total number of engagements by the total number of impressions.

Finally, organizations can gather even more data by clicking on a specific tweet to learn the exact kind of engagement that occurred. When each tweet is analyzed, brands can identify whether brand community members clicked a profile, clicked on a video or photo within the tweet, favorited a tweet, clicked links, replied, retweeted, or expanded the tweet in their stream to see more details.

*Followers*    The Followers overview tab shows the number of followers in an audience, the main interests of the audiences, occupation, gender, household income, net worth, consumer buying styles, and wireless carrier. In addition to the overview in the Followers section, there are also four other tabs that brands can review for more details: demographics, lifestyle, consumer behavior, or mobile footprint.

1.  Demographics provides information such as gender, education completed, household income, occupation, home type (such as single family, multi-family, or condominium), home value, preferred language, country, region, and marital status.
2.  Lifestyles provides information on the top interests and TV genres preferred by an audience.
3.  Consumer behavior provides information on the type of credit cards the brand community uses, aftermarket auto buyer types, consumer buying style, and consumer good purchases can be analyzed.
4.  Lastly, mobile footprint identifies which wireless carrier is most prominent among an audience. Brands can then compare their audience to another audience such as the general Twitter demographics or organic audiences.

*Twitter Cards*    Another important element in evaluating Twitter is the use of Twitter Cards, a method to add rich media into tweets with advanced tracking information in order to help drive traffic to a brand's website. In order to use Twitter cards, HTML code will need to be added to the website. There are four kinds of cards that can be used to enhance the tweets that link to content on a brand's own website:

1.  Summary Card: This is the default card that will include a title, description, and thumbnail and Twitter account attribution. Essentially, this card provides a preview of a web page prior to someone clicking on the link.

2.  Summary Card with Larger Image: This type of card has the same functionality as the summary card, but prominently displays an image, making it a strong choice for brands that have powerful visuals.
3.  App Card: This is designed to point people to a direct download of an app.
4.  Player Card: This is designed to provide media-rich experiences, such as playing a video or audio, for a brand's followers.

In addition to the metrics that are available on regular posts in Twitter, brands using Twitter Cards can also identify top influencers in order to recognize who they should engage with more, review the sources that the top influencers tweeted from, a rank of which pages had the most Twitter cards from the brand's website, and compare which kind of Twitter card is most effective among the brand audience. The information available from a Twitter card can be quite helpful in the evaluation of a campaign and the engagement that specific Twitter tactics were able to generate.

While many other platforms could be reviewed, the purpose of this chapter is not to serve as an exhaustive how-to for platform analytics, but rather to extrapolate the *kinds* of data that need to be gathered in the evaluation stage to develop a meaningful analysis of a campaign. Having reviewed Facebook Insights and Twitter analytics, two other platforms will help clarify the kinds of measurements that different social media platform genres opt to provide. Instagram, a visual platform, and YouTube, a video platform, will be briefly reviewed to illustrate the ways brands can obtain information from communities with visual and video content as the primary kind of posts.

## INSTAGRAM

As with many social platforms when they first launch, Instagram began without having an internal analytic option for brands. But as it developed and began offering advertising, it released access to analytic options in late 2014. Instagram's analytics allows organizations to determine which organic and paid content most resonates with their brand communities. Similar to Facebook and Twitter, the first metrics include a general overview of the last 28 days, showing impressions, reach, and a profile summary. Beneath that summary, week-by-week analysis is provided for the Instagram account. Within this portion of the analytic dashboard, brands can view the information for the week by reviewing: 1) performance, 2) audience, and 3) post analytic options. This allows brands to compare which type of content has the highest performance and resonates the most with a given audience. This information will provide helpful insight into which kinds of photos, approaches to images, and even style of presentation for graphics not only most resonate with a community but also seem to be most effective at creating two-way dialogue around campaign messages.

## YOUTUBE

As with other social media platforms, YouTube's analytics incorporates paid performance, such as details on revenue and income from ads that show on a channel, as well as tracking paid placement details. Brands can opt to filter and organize the organic metrics to understand how engagement on YouTube best works for non-paid campaign initiatives. A report that provides particularly meaningful measurements of YouTube engagement is located in the performance metrics, which indicates how engaged an audience was throughout a video by identifying elements like the length of time the video was watched and moments that seem to lose (or gain) audience interest. This level of information allows brands to identify the style and approach to videos that most resonate with an audience. Additionally, the engagement report provides base metrics on information about subscribers, thumbs-ups (or thumbs-downs), comments, and sharing for specific videos. Brands may review videos based on average number of views per video, time watched, total ratings, total engagement, and other metrics.

In addition to the analytic options provided by social media profiles, many brands opt for third-party social media dashboards that help track analytics across a variety of platforms. This can save time and also allows for other kinds of comparison across the platforms simultaneously. There are many options, both paid and free, that are available for brands looking for an integrated analytics option. Some of these platforms include Hootsuite, Sprout Social, Buffer, and SumAll. Google Analytics is also exceptionally powerful, and will be discussed later in this chapter as a way to evaluate social media engagement.

Social media professionals should understand that metrics on social sites reflect the primary values, purpose, and engagement capabilities of the social site—they are not all uniform, nor should they be. Each platform is unique and the analytics reflect that diversity. Social media experts, therefore, should understand how to make meaningful sense of the diversity of data and apply it to a single campaign's evaluation. The key concept to grasp, whether working with a specific social media platform analytic dashboard or a third-party option, is that brands need to be able to identify and measure meaningful communication in every social brand community. Remember, metrics are all about identifying *who* is doing *what* with *which* kinds of content, *when* it is happening, and *how* that supports the vision of the brand being on social media. Be sure, therefore, to carefully review the available platform metrics for any social media channel that is part of a campaign. Only after analyzing the capabilities and interaction functions of a platform will the brand be able to identify relevant data and apply it to the evaluation of a campaign.

With this brief overview of social media platform analytics, it is now possible to return to the larger discussion on how to use data from social media implementation and interaction and apply it in an effective way to the evaluation of a campaign.

## Message Reach

The goal of studying the message reach is to understand the exposure, or the potential audience size, a campaign message achieved. To help facilitate this evaluation of the message reach, reference the content calendar monitoring section where specific activities were recorded throughout the campaign and then review the messages in three different ways: 1) Individual posts; 2) Strategies; 3) Objectives.

First analyze each post and identify the reach, or how many people were exposed to the message. There should be a column next to each post within the content calendar that identified this information—if it is missing, go into the social media platform analytics and retrieve it. Second, sort the content calendar by specific strategies. It can be helpful to compare across strategies to see if exposure was given proportionally to all strategies or if certain ones had an average reach that was greater than others. This could provide context for why some may have been more effective and others seemed negligible. Third, do the same kind of comparison across objectives. The goal is to understand which specific posts and strategies had the strongest reach (and largest potential audience) and, ultimately, which objectives were given the greatest exposure.

---

### EXPERT INSIGHT

*Laurie Meacham*

**What do you think is one hallmark competency social media professionals need to succeed?**

Humanity! Don't forget that social is exactly that: social.

**What do you believe makes a social media campaign effective?**

In one word: engagement. If you're sharing content that your customers care about and want to engage with, you're probably being effective.

**How can social media professionals show the value of social media to an organization's bottom line efforts?**

Ultimately, the value created from social media efforts is one of loyalty.

**With the increased scrutiny on vanity metrics for social media evaluation, what would you identify as key values within social media that show authentic ROI for a brand?**

I believe it all comes down to loyalty. If you're able to connect with your Customers and maintain their loyalty through the relationship you've built with them on social media, then you're definitely getting an authentic ROI. Regardless of how many likes, shares, RTs, etc. you get, if your Customers are doing more business with you and sharing their personal experiences with your brand with their network, then you're achieving success.

**In what ways, if any, is it possible to assess the value added by social media to the quality of relationships with key audiences?**

This is a hard thing to measure, but the important thing is to remain authentic to your brand. No one should be portraying their brand or business differently on social than they do at any other touch point. All interactions should be reflective of the brand and social is just another channel where it's possible to engage and leave an impression. If those opportunities are genuine and used wisely, they'll add to the overall value of the customer experience.

**What do you think makes social media evaluation or measurement so intimidating? Is there a way around this intimidation factor?**

I think there's a tendency to look for reassurance that the effort we're putting into social media is the means to an end, but it's really an ongoing effort, it's an ongoing development of a relationship. Social media is a unique touchpoint in that you have an opportunity to engage with customers, often outside of a transaction. There's not always an immediate ROI, it can be hard to quantify success, but when you look at human nature, patterns, and behavior, it all comes down to knowing that there's a unique opportunity here to humanize a brand and connect with people in a way that's meaningful to them. The way around the intimidation factor is knowing that there are a lot of ways to define success when it comes to social media—and they all might be right, in their own way.

**What value does evaluation provide for a social media team and organization as a whole?**

There are certainly some metrics that are valuable. To use a very simple example, my team has a goal of maintaining an average response time of 10 minutes. Not to say that we respond to every mention, but for the ones we do respond to, we want to make it quick. That's the expectation of our customers and it's something that shows we're here, and we're listening. Ultimately, it's our goal of inspiring humanity that drives evaluation like that. We always ask the question: are we doing the right things for the right reasons?

**Connect with Laurie:** @laurieameacham

*Laurie Meacham is the Manager of Customer Commitment and Social Media for JetBlue Airways*

## Engagement

While exposure is helpful to understand, it means very little if an audience did not interact with the content or engage in the conversation on social media. Therefore, measuring the nature and depth of engagement is also crucial. To perform this evaluation, it is helpful to divide the social media posts by platform and save them in separate files or tabs within an Excel document for ease of analysis and interpretation. This allows brands to customize each report based on engagement types within a given platform. Next, add columns for each kind of engagement that can be measured in a platform, such as likes in Facebook, or thumbs-ups in YouTube, or comments in Instagram. Be sure to include a "total engagement" column for the platform. As was done for message reach, evaluate the engagement for each post, each strategy, and each objective. Provide feedback on the most effective and least effective posts, strategies, and objectives by each platform.

### TWO-WAY DIALOGUE AUDIT

In addition to understanding whether the content that was delivered reached the audiences and was well-received, as indicated through comments, sharing, and interaction, it is important to evaluate the implementation of two-way conversations by conducting a summative, two-way dialogue audit. Because social media is about a dialogue, brands should regularly evaluate the capacity and performance of brand engagement during a campaign. Chuck Hemann and Ken Burbary (2013) suggest that there are two levels of measurement within the two-way dialogue audit: conversations within the social media properties that a brand owns and conversations outside of the direct social network of the brand. The necessary measurements and analysis for each of these levels will be discussed below.

*Conversations in the Brand's Own Social Media Platforms*    Whenever content is posted onto social media, there is the potential that a member of the audience will comment, mention, follow, or share via their own social media channels. In order to have high levels of community interaction, therefore, a brand cannot simply post original content, but they must also *respond* when the community interacts. Review posts to see if there are unanswered questions or comments, whether the brand replied to new members who joined as a result of the initiative, and whether there are any pieces of interaction that seem dropped. It could be that the level of interaction is far too high to reply to all community members. In this case, it is important to identify whether there was a process in place to understand how dialogue would be handled: were all influencers responded to? Were complaints addressed? Were questions answered? Identify the process for how the brand responded and then analyze the interaction based on the process.

Two-way dialogue audits should also review the social community's participation in the conversation or dialogue. There are several steps to effectively analyze community participation. Four key components are recommended by social media expert, Avinash Kaushik (2011):

1. conversation rate
2. amplification rate
3. applause rate
4. economic value.

He suggested this model because he wanted to "propose a framework you can use to measure success using metrics that matter for one simple reason: They actually measure if you are participating in the channel in an optimal fashion" (para. 6).

Measuring a *conversation rate*, the rate at which conversations happen within the social platform, provides a base estimate of the effectiveness of the engagement with a brand community. In order to measure the conversation rate, simply provide the number of comments, replies, or other conversation pieces per post. Whenever a social media community member generated original content in the conversation, it should be included as part of the conversation rate.

Next, evaluate the *amplification* of the conversation. This involves looking specifically at things that elevated the conversation into a wider audience, such as shares or retweets. Kaushik suggests that this type of activity helps break past the limitations of an online community size (for example, 50,000 followers on Twitter), and into a wider audience network of engagement. Over time, those people in the wider network, which Kaushik identifies as second-level and third-level networks, may become part of the brand's direct social media community due to discovering relevant and meaningful content produced by the brand through amplification by community members. While this metric does not measure a two-way dialogue with the community, it does show amplification of a conversation that was being fostered in social media, which can eventually produce more two-way dialogues.

Third, *applause* is a way to measure the affinity of the community with a post. This involves likes, favorites, +1s, and other affirmation-based actions in social media. This is valuable as it allows the organization to identify what kind of content is most valuable to an audience. In addition, it builds credibility of the content as users provide endorsements. This will help attract other users who are interested in the same content. Kaushik (2011) identifies the value of this kind of interaction saying, "Your selfless social media contribution comes back to assist you in driving valuable business outcomes" ("3. Applause Rate," para. 15).

Finally, *economic value* should be calculated, and this will be discussed in greater detail below. It is worth noting that using social media for the sole purpose of driving bottom-line business revenue will not necessarily yield a strong social strategy. Social media is about being *social*. It involves developing relationships, contributing to conversations, and being an active participant in an online community that shares a mutual interest. But that does not mean that social media cannot support bottom-line initiatives. Kaushik argues, "Social media participation, done right, adds value to the company's bottom-line. Some of it can't be computed. That is okay. But some of it can be and it is your job, nay duty (!), to quantify that" ("Economic Value," para. 10).

Having analyzed participation in the conversation, it is important to next evaluate the increase in positive communication that occurred as a result of the campaign. To evaluate this, it is helpful to run a new share of voice (SOV) report that highlights activity during the social media campaign and compares it to the original share of voice report that was developed in the listening phase. Remember, SOV involves looking at key competitors and calculating how much conversation relates to the brand versus competitor brands.

In addition to the SOV report, there are several more layers that can be analyzed in evaluation to understand the full impact of the dialogue throughout a social media campaign. For example, a "share of conversation" report could be developed. Chuck Hemann and Ken Burbary (2013) define share of conversation as "a more accurate gauge of how aware people are of a product or campaign within a broader industry than share of voice. This metric tracks, typically in percentage form, how much conversation is happening versus the broader industry" (p. 21). *Share of conversation* reports reflect what topics a brand community is talking about, and how many of those conversations reference or mention the brand in any way, whereas a share of voice report focuses more on a comparison of conversations that mention the brand versus conversations that mention competition. In short, share of conversation focuses on topics and the brand, whereas share of voice focuses on competition and the brand. Share of voice takes a topic, such as fitness, and analyzes all of the conversations happening on a platform about that topic. Then, the brand calculates how much, if any, of the conversation about fitness relates to the brand.

Other dimensions to conversations that can be helpful to evaluate include the sentiment of conversations taking place, the resonance (or how well the brand community is accepting a message), and the overall volume (or how frequently communication is occurring) of the brand's conversation in social media. To calculate any of these, a brand should analyze each post and interaction within a brand community, using many of the same tools discussed in Chapter 2, on listening. Then, beyond merely *counting* the mentions, comments, or tweets, each one should be analyzed for the tone that the brand community had in interaction, for the resonance (indicated by the conversation rate, amplification, and applause), and for the frequency of the brand's communication within the dialogue. These measurements can then be compared and contrasted to provide a fuller analysis of why certain strategies, tactics, or posts were successful in supporting the campaign objectives and others may not have been. For example, perhaps there was a high level of interaction around a post, but the tone was fairly negative. This may show why, despite having high scores in engagement, the strategy was not, in fact, supported through that interaction. Or, perhaps the brand seemed to be strong (having a louder volume) sometimes within a campaign, but then was quiet for long periods in other places. That may have sent mixed messages to the community regarding the brand's intentionality with dialogue and genuine interest in conversations. These kinds of analyses help provide context and meaning for the overall impact of the campaign.

*Conversations Outside the Brand's Own Social Media Platforms*   The second level of conversation analysis deals with those interactions occurring outside of the brand's own social media platforms. Throughout a campaign, there are often conversations that are relevant for the brand but may not directly mention the brand or may even incorrectly tag the organization. Review interactions that occurred from the brand during the campaign that were *unrelated* to a specific post by the brand, perhaps examining interactions by the brand around certain hashtags that were relevant or providing resources and answers to social media user questions that had nothing to do with planned posts from the content calendar. Look at these conversations to determine if the interactions seem well received. Do this by asking questions such as: was the brand perceived as helpful or intrusive, based on the response of the social media user? Were any actions triggered as a result of the communication with the person (such as liking a page, having issues resolved, etc.)? Ideally, the brand should join appropriate conversations beyond the social media posts that the organization crafted itself. This second level of evaluation analyzes whether, throughout the campaign, the brand was able to appropriately join conversations that were user-generated within the social sphere and yet outside of the original content posted by the brand for the campaign.

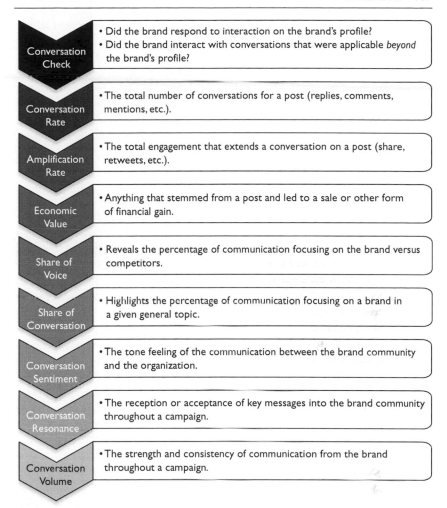

**Conversation Check**
- Did the brand respond to interaction on the brand's profile?
- Did the brand interact with conversations that were applicable *beyond* the brand's profile?

**Conversation Rate**
- The total number of conversations for a post (replies, comments, mentions, etc.).

**Amplification Rate**
- The total engagement that extends a conversation on a post (share, retweets, etc.).

**Economic Value**
- Anything that stemmed from a post and led to a sale or other form of financial gain.

**Share of Voice**
- Reveals the percentage of communication focusing on the brand versus competitors.

**Share of Conversation**
- Highlights the percentage of communication focusing on a brand in a given general topic.

**Conversation Sentiment**
- The tone feeling of the communication between the brand community and the organization.

**Conversation Resonance**
- The reception or acceptance of key messages into the brand community throughout a campaign.

**Conversation Volume**
- The strength and consistency of communication from the brand throughout a campaign.

*Figure 6.4* Components to Communication Audits

ADVERTISING METRICS

While this text largely focuses on running organic social media campaigns, the integration of paid strategies is a reality for many social media initiatives. When a campaign integrates paid placement, it is essential that evaluation of those placements occurs. As was mentioned above, many social media platforms offer comparative evaluations between organic and paid posts on a site. In addition, social media advertising platforms offer deeper analytics that relate to various pricing and interaction methods such as cost per click (CPC), cost per impression (CPM), cost per view (CPV), or cost per action (CPA). Each advertising platform provides different combinations of these pricing methods. As an advertising strategy is implemented, analysis should be provided on the effectiveness of the placement, the value of the clicks or followers that are gained through the advertising efforts, and feedback on whether such efforts should continue, be adjusted and then continue, or be discontinued as part of the ongoing support to reach a campaign's objective. For the final evaluation, review the total contribution of the paid placement efforts in social media toward the success of the objective the strategy was designed to support. It is helpful to analyze what percentage of the success should be attributed to paid efforts versus organic efforts.

## Impact

The final level of evaluation has to do with the end results of the campaign. This portion involves returning to the SMART, outcome-based objectives that were established at the beginning of the campaign and analyzing whether or not these objectives were accomplished. This is why it is so crucial that each objective is designed to be specific (so brands know what to measure) and measurable (so brands know what change they are expecting to see in metrics). In addition, the time elements of the objective allow brands to know when the measurement should take place. For each objective, provide the exact social metrics that confirm success or show the need to improve. Sometimes, the data that is needed to determine whether an objective was met is unavailable as part of the typical social media dashboards. This requires social media professionals to review information from the website analytics of an organization, often integrating platforms like Google Analytics into the evaluation.

### Integrated Social Media Measurement

As previously mentioned, there are some metrics that are housed outside of a social media platform, yet they are crucial to knowing the value of social media initiatives. Often, these types of metrics involve conversion behaviors that are ultimately tracked on the website of an organization. To find and mine this type of data, coordination with the website team is required.

A critical part of the process in designing campaign budgets is to assign values to specific activities. For example, if lead generation was the focus of the campaign, how much is each name worth? Or, perhaps the campaign was designed to generate awareness for a topic or cause. How much value is assigned to each person who received or is exposed to the information? Typically the marketing department would be able to provide these values. If those values were not already established, the social media team should coordinate with the marketing department to determine the value before launching the campaign. The question then becomes how to attribute an action on a website, such as gaining a lead for a sale, to social media engagement.

To address these kinds of questions, use the organization's website analytics.

There is a wealth of information and data that the website analytics should be able to provide, including the ability to track user paths, traffic sources and conversions. Perhaps one of the most valuable competencies that a social media professional can apply to this final stage of the campaign is recognizing which data is helpful and which is a distraction. Lars Lofgren (n.d.), KISSmetrics Marketing Analyst, argues,

> Not all data is helpful. Some of it is worse than worthless because it tricks us into believing we have answers when we don't. But when you focus on data that helps you make decisions, everything else in your business gets easier.
>
> (para. 3)

The goal is to identify actionable metrics that inform decisions and future strategy (Lofgren, n.d., "Actionable Metrics"). Jay Baer (2013) suggests that the type of numbers, or metrics, that matter can be classified into four genres:

1. Consumption metrics, which are the engagement data points gathered from social media dashboards such as watched videos, reach, or visits.
2. Advocacy and sharing metrics, also gathered from social dashboards, which indicate that the content was shared through actions such as retweets, share buttons, or quote directly.
3. Lead-generation metrics, which indicates that someone wants to learn more or is considering a purchase.
4. Sales metrics, which indicates that revenue was earned as a result of an action taken.

While consumption metrics and advocacy/sharing metrics are easier to find and are, therefore, regularly highlighted by organizations, it is also critical to dive deeper into the data in order to measure the lead-generation and sales metrics (pp. 174–181).

Recognizing that analytics will give far more data than is useful, it is necessary for the social media team to identify the specific information that is required to measure objectives. In many analytic programs, a customized dashboard can be established that will track specific data, which has been identified as useful, from social media sources. This filtered data will help the social media team to collect and track the most important data pieces that relate to their campaign. Be thoroughly familiar with the analytic data available prior to beginning evaluation in order to correctly assess what data will be most meaningful and actionable.

One helpful feature in analytics is customization of a URL so that it can be tracked and associated with specific efforts. Some people use third-party apps to shorten and track URLs, such as Bitly and Ow.ly. These services allow brands to shorten a URL and then track whether people end up clicking the link. One thing that these services cannot do, however, is tell a brand what a user does *after* clicking the link. While it may not seem to be crucial information, it really is valuable insight, particularly when driving people from a brand's social media platform to the brand's website. The ability for the social media team to definitively answer what social media brand members do when they visit the website helps support the claim that social media engagement resulted in lead-generation or sale metrics on the brand's website.

To develop a customized URL that can be tracked by analytic software, brands identify specific data pieces to include in the URL so that the analytics system knows to track the information. A brand can identify a specific medium that the link was sending people from, the campaign that the link was associated with, the source for where the link was located, and the type of content or term that was included to drive an individual to visit a brand's website. Analytic platforms make the process of creating custom URLs quite easy. Google Analytics, for example, provides a page to help brands generate custom URLs that will be tracked in Google Analytics and provide reports on that activity. On this page, brands can simply copy and paste the URL that they want to put onto social media, such as a link to a product that is on sale or a free trial to sign up for, and then enter the exact information they want to track (such as the name of the campaign or the source, such as the social media platform, that will be driving the traffic). Google Analytics will then generate a custom URL for the social media team to use, track, and analyze.

A custom URL a brand might develop, for example, could be for all links that will be posted on Facebook with the intention of driving people to sign up for a free trial of a product. The website analytics would then track what those users who click the link in Facebook do when they arrive on the brand's website. Social media strategists will be able to know whether the users sign up for the trial, whether they look at the page and immediately leave, or if they end up signing up and also looking around at other pages. This kind of information helps a social media team gain much more insight on a social media brand community's behavior. In addition to monitoring the activity of people who click to visit the website from Facebook, the team may also opt to create another custom URL that is used only for Twitter. This new custom URL would also drive people to the free trial, but would be customized with tracking information to identify that those individuals came to the website from Twitter as opposed to Facebook. In the evaluation, then, the team could compare the effectiveness of Twitter in driving sign-ups versus Facebook. It would be possible not only to understand which platform drove the most sign-ups, but also

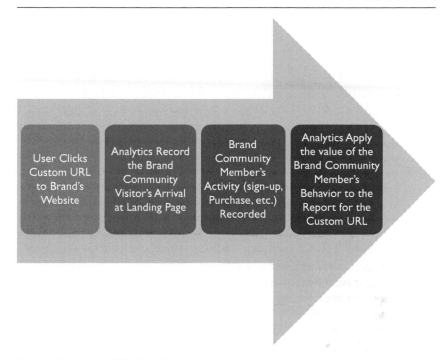

*Figure 6.5* Custom URL Data Tracking Process

which platform was most likely to send users who viewed other pages on the website, people who would spend a longer time on the website, and those who were not interested in the content and immediately left.

This concept of creating custom URLs to track the behavior of users from social media could be applied across platforms such as incorporating a custom URL for Pinterest, Instagram, or YouTube, or even incorporated to test specific *types* of posts in a platform. By creating two custom URLs, the social media team would be able to measure whether video posts in Facebook or photo posts in Facebook drove more sign-ups. Similarly, it would be possible to compare whether videos posted in Twitter, Instagram, or Facebook were most influential. Therefore, using separate custom URLs across platforms and for different post types allows the brand to compare and contrast the effectiveness of posts in actually producing tangible results such as lead-generation or sales on the brand's website.

Whether brands use custom URLs for each social media platform (such as one for Twitter, one for Facebook, one for Pinterest), have custom URLs for each *type* of post analyzed by platforms (such as Facebook links with images, Facebook links with videos, etc.), or even if custom URLs are generated for specific strategies, to determine which is most effective, this method of tracking allows brands to analyze every user who clicks on a link and accurately measure their behavioral actions on the brand's website. In conclusion, the goal within this level of analytics is to: 1) identify the type of action or behavior that needs to be tracked within social media; 2) develop the back-end process to track the action (customized URL, analytic report, etc.); and 3) pull the data at the end of the campaign to directly attribute concrete actions that resulted as part of a social media campaign effort.

### Outcome-Based Objectives and Reporting

Whether using proprietary analytic software, Google Analytics, or using a mixture of paid and free social and web analytics tools, the ultimate goals are the same: identify meaningful data, apply the information to the campaign objectives, and evaluate the effectiveness of a campaign. Having SMART, outcome-based objectives should allow for precise evaluation of an objective's success or lack thereof. It is also important for a social media professional to dive deeper into the data and apply *context* to the success or failure of the objective. This occurs when each of the three layers of evaluation (preparation, implementation, and impact) are considered.

Additionally, because analytic and reporting platforms offer automatic downloads of many of the reports, it is quite tempting to simply export those reports, compile them together, and send them as one document to management. It is best, however, for a social media strategist to customize reports and provide the appropriate context. Although automated reports can provide useful additions to a social media report for a campaign, a strategist should fully review each level of the evaluation (preparation, implementation, and impact), provide KPIs from those key areas, and then offer a comprehensive analysis of the campaign's effectiveness as a whole. It is helpful to include a one- or two-page executive summary at the beginning of a social media evaluation report so that those who are unable to dive into all the information can still assess the value of the social media campaign. It is also equally important for the report to break down each stage of the campaign, highlighting strengths, identifying weaknesses, and ultimately reflecting on the goals being met. Finally, each evaluation of a social media campaign should include recommendations, lessons learned, and key take-away points that can be applied to a better strategy and more effective campaign design in the future.

## The Future of Social Media Campaigns

The nature of social media is that it is constantly changing, evolving, and moving. Being effective in social media requires that brands regularly adapt. Social media compels professionals to be bold, to be willing to attempt new processes, and to adopt new platforms and strategies. The four steps to a social media campaign provide a framework that professionals can apply to brand initiatives in the ever-shifting social world. The value of listening, understanding the culture of a brand and the current social media climate, is paramount for any campaign. This in-depth information infuses life into the efforts and activity of the brand. Meaningful data is precisely how brands develop strategic campaigns— they form *out* of research that seeks to understand the social media brand community. The strategic design step marries the science of data with the art of relationship, drawing together all of the information into a creative and engaging roadmap that guides the social media efforts of the brand. After the creation of this social masterpiece, the third step, implementation, orchestrates the tapestry of engagement, weaving together all the strategies and tactics into a harmonious dialogue with key stakeholders. It is in this step, the implementation of a campaign, that many brands struggle to understand how interaction can ever be scripted. After all, social media requires flexibility and adaptation. The beauty behind data-informed strategic designs, however, is that they are developed not from a static, boring room full of people who are bent on pushing messages in front of the public but rather grow as a direct result of understanding *who* the brand community is, what they *value,* and the conversations they *want* to be having with the brand. Campaigns developed from this type of relationally informed data are anything but scripted—they are, in fact, *reactive,* responding to the needs and communication of the brand community connections. In addition, the third step of a campaign involves not only sharing content from the brand that was developed around a rigorous understanding of the audience, but also *actively* responding to the live-time interaction, discussions, and questions that occur throughout the life of a campaign. Strategic design is preparation for dynamic conversations and thriving relationships in brand communities, not staunch parameters that stifle the relational dimension to social media. Finally, the fourth step evaluates all of the efforts of a campaign, analyzing everything from the smallest piece of information to the overall impact. This analysis not only provides insight into the impact of the campaign, elements that supported that success and areas that hindered it, but also affords rich data for future social media use. In this sense, social media campaigns are heuristic in nature, in that each campaign reveals new information about the brand community and the relationships that key stakeholders have with the brand. This valuable insight should not be lost by using it solely to evaluate a single campaign and then filing away. Rather, it should also be used to apply strategic insight into future campaigns.

The relationships in social media with the brand community do not end with each campaign. They are, ideally, long-term, ongoing relationships that will span the course of many campaigns, initiatives, and efforts. Losing the insight gained about these relationships, the ways people interact and respond, tactics that are particularly helpful in building meaningful dialogue, and the methods in which the brand community has developed over a course of a campaign would be tragic. Rather, this wealth of information should be carefully secured and purposefully integrated into future campaigns. Not only is this simply a smart move on the part of a brand, giving them a wealth of information for the next campaign, it is also a sign of the value that the brand community holds. If these relationships matter, genuinely, to the brand, then it is a disservice to disregard every conversation and interaction at the end of a campaign, to simply begin again. Authentic relationships are a continual dance of communication, interaction, and engagement.

The core component of social media is people: understanding them, interacting with them, and developing relationships with them. Ultimately, the goal of strategic social media use is to encourage purposeful engagement in the midst of a dynamic platform that fosters unscripted, two-way dialogue. In conclusion, while there are four steps to a social media campaign, and this framework provides a structure to have robust and authentic relationships in social media, the truth is the four steps never stop—instead, they form a continuous process, devoted to thriving relationships and authentic communication. Once evaluation concludes, the brand should already begin again, listening, seeking to understand, and preparing meaningful communication with their brand community.

## KEY CONCEPT SNAPSHOT

1. Evaluation contains many components that are designed to explore the total impact and effectiveness of each element within a campaign. While evaluating the SMART, outcome-based objectives should be the key measurement of success, professionals should also analyze all elements included within the preparation, implementation, and impact, to understand what contributed to or hindered the overall effectiveness of a campaign.

2. Many brands rely on vanity metrics to illustrate the value of their social presence. Rigorous evaluation demands that social media professionals analyze KPIs that have a direct connection to the purpose of the campaign and the two-way engagement being sustained within social media.

3. Social media evaluation is not something that happens in a vacuum. Often, coordination with the marketing, IT, and web teams will be required for a truly holistic understanding of the impact of social media within an organization.

4. Evaluation is never the end of social media interaction—rather, it serves as the start to the process for the next campaign. Relationships are continual, as is interaction in social media. Strategic design recognizes the value and contribution past campaigns make to future social media initiatives.

## Suggested Reading

Hemann, C., & Burbary, K. (2013). *Digital marketing analytics: Making sense of consumer data in a digital world*. Indianapolis, IN: Que.

Kelly, N. (2013). *How to measure social media: A step-by-step guide to developing and assessing social media ROI*. Indianapolis, IN: Que.

Paine, K. (2011). *Measure what matters: Online tools for understanding customers, social media, engagement, and key relationships*. Hoboken, NJ: Wiley.

## References

*Note*: All website URLs accessed February 4, 2016.

Baer, J. (2013). *Youtility: Why smart marketing is about help not hype*. New York: Portfolio/Penguin.

Blanchard, O. (2011). *Social media ROI: Managing and measuring social media efforts in your organization* [E-reader version]. Indianapolis, IN: Que.

Broom, G., & Sha, B. L. (2013). *Cutlip and Center's effective public relations*. Boston: Pearson.

Hemann, C., & Burbary, K. (2013). *Digital marketing analytics: Making sense of consumer data in a digital world*. Indianapolis, IN: Que.

Kaushik, A. (2011, Oct. 10). Best social media metrics: Conversation, amplification, applause, economic value. *Occam's Razor*. Retrieved from: www.kaushik. net/avinash/best-social-media-metrics-conversation-amplification-applause-economic-value/

Lofgren, L. (n.d.). Metrics, metrics on the wall, who's the vainest of them all? *KissMetrics Blog*. Retrieved from: https://blog.kissmetrics.com/vainest-metrics/

Paine, K. (2011). *Measure what matters: Online tools for understanding customers, social media, engagement, and key relationships*. Hoboken, NJ: Wiley.

Peterson, E. (2006, Jan. 1). *The big book of key performance indicators*. Eric T. Peterson. Retrieved from: http://design4interaction.com/wp-content/uploads/2012/09/The_Big_Book_of_Key_Performance_Indicators_by_Eric_Peterson.pdf

Sterne, J. (2010). *Social media metrics: How to measure and optimize your marketing investment*. Hoboken, NJ: John Wiley & Sons.

# Index